MONEY
UNIVERSITY

CASH MATTHEWS

aBM

Money University
"The Book"

Published by:
A Book's Mind
PO Box 272847
Fort Collins, CO 80527

In Partnership with: Solomon Publishing
A Wholly Owned Subsidiary of Money University, LLC.

Copyright 2015
ISBN: 978-1-939828-44-6

Technical Editor: Barbara Engle

Technical Contributors: Robert Greene, Harvey and Betsy Kitzman

Edited by Barbara Engle and Autumn Fowlkes

Contributors: Jennifer Eskina, Barbara Engle, Autumn Fowlkes, Ben Randle

Advisory Council: David Temple, Ben Randle, Barbara Engle, Robert Greene, Jennifer
Eskina, Timothy Nieto, Ric Cordle, Marc Carlson, Craig Robinson, Rebekah Frost,
Sharell Eason, Cathy Ruiz, Joe Bowen, Brian Catalano, Gary Motal, Gary Beasley,
Veronica Morgan, Paul and Linnea Danna, Jackie and Sue Mills, Simon Lambert, Parc
Smith, Steven and Randi Babcock, Andrew Corre, and Timothy Schaffner

Life Contributors: Katy Matthews, Geraldine Hart, Dorothy Rogers, Joy Hylton,
Charles Matthews, Carey Matthews, Chris Ann Dale

Project Editor: Amanda Kimmerly

Printed In The U.S.A. On Regular Paper. God Bless America And Her People

Table of Contents

Important Disclaimer

In the course of *Money University, Money University: The Student Book,* and *Money University: The Teachers Guide,* you will see and read many different possible rates of interest related to investment or savings returns. These examples may NOT exist in real life or in anyone else's life. They are hypothetical and ONLY for the purpose of education and example. These examples should NOT be relied on to make financial decisions and are NOT factual.

For my hard-headed friends and family: the interest rates mentioned in this book are not real numbers pulled from any factual place. They are used merely for interpretation of possibilities of growth at a particular rate of return. These do not estimate, predict, guarantee, nor suggest a possible rate of return on any particular type of account. Investing takes skill, money, time, guidance, and other factors. When you invest, you may lose all of your money. Visit with your licensed advisor, CPA, attorney, Swami, Pastor, or other trusted advisor BEFORE making any financial decisions.

Legal Disclaimer:

Information presented is for educational purposes only and does not intend to make an offer or solicitation for the sale or purchase of any specific securities product, service, or investment strategy. Investments involve risk and unless otherwise stated, are not guaranteed. Be sure to first consult with a qualified financial adviser, tax professional, or attorney before implementing any strategy or recommendation discussed herein.

For My Girls.

Chapter One
Why This Book Is Important
to Your Financial Success

Rule: What You Do Speaks So Loudly, I Cannot Hear What You Say . . .
Actions Speak Louder Than Words . . .

Congratulations! Do YOU know what day this is? Come on, think about it! Today—this exact moment—is the five-year anniversary of EXACTLY five years ago! And five years ago, where did you think you would be **right now**? Did your plan work? Have you encountered some resistance to your goals, perhaps? Did your financial life work out the way you imagined? More importantly, are you living a life that you are satisfied with?

Perhaps you are just getting started in life. Maybe your journey is just beginning, and **Money University** is the first road map to success that you have ever opened. Either way, getting started toward something you desire can be exciting, scary, confusing, and wonderful all in the same moment! Regardless of your position in life, there is never a bad time to learn something new.

At the age of twenty-one, I was pretty excited to play my first round of golf. What an awesome game. It has so many moving parts, just like money does. It rewards consistency; it punishes when you play in the weeds. It can leave you feeling mystified, humiliated, and frustrated beyond belief. It can also be pretty awesome when you get it right!

That first year I began to play, I had a HUGE breakthrough. I was scoring around 100 consistently when a nice fellow with an awesome moustache walked up to me while I was practicing on the golf range. He mentioned to me that if I held the club in a particular way and stood a particular way, that the ball would behave for me in a more *predictable* fashion. BOOM! Within my first year, I went from being a 100 shooter to shooting in the 70's.

Being able to operate the machinery made ALL THE DIFFERENCE! I look back on that single moment of advice as a *turning point* for me in my golf life. Now, thirty years later, I can look back and be thankful not just **FOR** the advice, but that I actually **TOOK** the advice, practiced the advice, and then benefitted **greatly** from it.

EDITOR'S NOTE:
The author is a golf nut and may include these kinds
of stories frequently.... CASH!! Get to the point!!!

Oh, sorry. Okay, money—statistically, for most people—can be confusing. Earning money, investing money, saving money, paying taxes on money, giving money away, all of these concepts may pose a real threat to your mental health. And what about that pesky market? Is it going up or down today? And these kids of mine, how should I teach them about money? Won't their teachers do that? It is enough to make me want to . . . read a book on money and get educated! This is **that** book.

We live in the USA, where we are blessed to have nearly-limitless opportunity. And yet, despite this great freedom, the statistics for the average working-American family is not so boastful. Consider this fact:

WE MAKE MILLIONS DURING OUR LIFETIMES,
BUT KEEP VERY LITTLE OF IT!

If we're making that kind of money, why aren't we all millionaires yet?

Let's take a simple and fun test.
We call it the Vomit Test:

1. How many years have you worked? _____years

2. What was your average annual family income? $_____

3. Multiply years x income to get lifetime income $_____
(This is the amount of money you have made in your lifetime!)

4. How much of that number do you have left in cash assets:
(Don't count home equity just yet) $_____

Does your number make you want to vomit?

If you have been an excellent saver and your test number doesn't alarm you, I want to personally congratulate you on good habits and good choices. I hope you will continue your march toward a successful financial life for you and your family. Our country needs MORE people like YOU!

If you haven't done a great job, welcome to the silent majority in the USA. Most people—despite making millions of dollars over a lifetime—are broke. In fact, 74% of the population that is past the age of sixty-five, lives below our nation's stated poverty line of $23,400.

With the average Social Security check being about $1,320 per month, you sort of come to an understanding that saving money is very important for your own financial future.

> **"I freed a thousand slaves. I could have freed a thousand more if only they knew they were slaves." —Harriet Tubman**

Harriet Tubman's quote is one for the ages. It illustrated her frustration of the time where she couldn't help people because they did not realize they needed help. One of the most difficult tasks is to cause somebody who—by all appearances is doing okay—to take a candid look at their financial situation. It is sort of like that old joke *"A guy jumps out of a thirty-story building. Halfway down, somebody yells out, "How you doing?" And the jumper replies, "So far so good!"* At the moment, most of us feel okay—as long as we're getting by and living indoors, we think we're doing *"pretty good."* The fact is that most of us are headed toward a desperate situation. The fact is without understanding the value placed on time, the values we place on **_money_** will always be substantially less. It isn't always that we're bad with money. The fact is most of us are bad with **_time_**.

Throw in a little bit of economic turmoil, and a whole bunch of time wasting, and **that** my friend is the absolute recipe for economic disaster! Oh, by the way, jumping out of a thirty-story window doesn't kill you. It is the harsh landing at the end that gets you every time. Take a moment of honest appraisal right this moment and answer this question: *"**_Am I headed toward a harsh landing_**?"*

> In the richest, most educated country in the history of the world, three out of four families live bleak economic lives past the age of sixty-five, DESPITE earning MILLIONS during their lifetimes.

This is simply not right. Surely there is something that each of us can do to alter the outcome of a lifetime where we earn millions yet live on pennies and struggle to survive. It is up to <u>YOU</u> to take a stand and speak up for yourself. It is <u>YOUR</u> responsibility to keep your economic engine finely tuned and running for a lifetime.

What you spend your money on is your economic-priority list. Truly, look at your budget. Your priorities are right there. Look at what you spend your money on. How much do you spend on your cell phones, internet, and cable television all added up together? Do that number in your mind. How much? $250? $300? Are you spending that same amount on making sure you retire well or become financially independent some day? If not, your cell phone and internet are YOUR priority, not wealth or ample retirement.

Technology has become your economic priority. How do you feel about that?

We ought to worry about our economic necessities. Do your economic priorities match up with your economic necessities? Do your expenses on economic priorities solve your most basic economic goals? Are you sleeping better because of the money you're spending on your economic priorities? Is your family better off because you are spending money on your economic priorities? Is it possible that placing such a high value on cell phones and internet and cable has caused us as a nation to ignore our actual responsibilities with our dollars? If you spend more money on your cell phone, internet, and cable TV than you do on your personal financial plan, you could be headed for a crash.

What would you be willing to do to ensure that your family survives financially? Are there decisions you would be willing to make and stand by in order to provide for you and your family's well being? If you took the Vomit Test and "failed," have you carefully identified the problem? Many of you still think you are bad with money. As we mentioned above, it may not be money that you need help with; it is usually time.

The Time-Value of Money

Let's say your parents decide to start a retirement plan for you **the day you were born**. There aren't many financial companies marketing to the newborn-baby retirement market. Why is that? Few, if any, seriously begin the retirement conversation until MUCH later in life. When did YOU start? Here is a fun example using just $1 per day for the first eighteen years of a child's life, then left to accumulate until the age of seventy, assuming an uninterrupted investment rate of 9% per year: (PLEASE SEE ALL DISCLAIMERS…THIS IS NOT INVESTMENT ADVICE. THIS IS A HYPOTHETICAL SITUATION THAT MAY NOT BE POSSIBLE IN YOUR OWN LIFE).

Summary: Your parents save $1 per day for you up until the *day you are eighteen. Then, those dollars that were saved are put away until* your age of seventy. That's it: a buck a day for eighteen years, then leave it alone until retirement. *Is this an idea that people should hear about and take action on?* Yep. Yes. *Sí. Tak. Ja.* You Betcha. Uh Huh.

Whatever language you speak, let's get started!

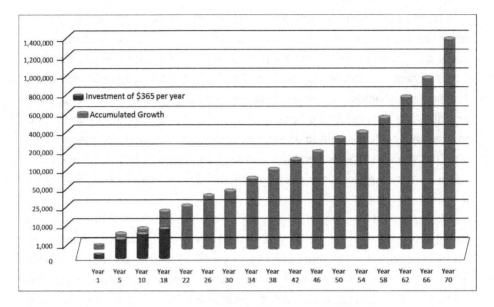

Legend within chart:
- Investment of $365 per year
- Accumulated Growth

($365 for 18 years) @ 9% = $15,074.

$15,074 left for fifty-two more years with no more investment deposits until age seventy when the baby retires = $1,331,787.

Summary: Your parents save a dollar a day all of your life until your age of eighteen. It grows at 9% annually. You wisely choose to leave it there until your retirement. Boom! $1,331,787.

Growing up, my grandmother, Geraldine, was always there with sage advice and lifelong wisdom to help me out. She had a long list of things that she thought I should consider as I developed into an adult. Here are the top five things my grandmother taught me as a child that continually benefit me today:

1. Eat your vegetables
2. Make your bed
3. Look both ways before crossing the street
4. Your dog will love you no matter what
5. Every little extra $1,331,787 will come in handy during retirement!

Even my grandmother enjoyed the wisdom of the ages. And of course, she is right. Every extra million dollars you have a retirement will indeed come in handy. Let's take a look at how most normal people do it:

Let's say we **don't** begin saving until we're forty years old. Perhaps we have a goal that just happens to be $1,331,787 by the age of seventy. That leaves us just thirty years to accomplish our goal. That's right; we have just thirty years to accomplish this humongous goal. To put that into another perspective, it means that we have only 360 more paychecks before we quit working and live on our savings! If we could accomplish a 9% rate of return each year from the age of forty until seventy, how much money would we have to put away each month to accomplish our goal of $1,331,787? The answer? We would be required to save $814 every single month for 30 years!

In the first example of saving a dollar a day until we are eighteen, we contributed a total of $6,570 to our long-term savings account. In the second example, we waited until age forty to get started; we had to contribute $293,094 to get the same result. Ask yourself, what is the difference?

The ANSWER: BETTER USE OF TIME!

See, we Americans are not bad with **money;** we are bad with **time**. Which one would you be more likely to contribute—$6,570 or $293,000? Are you starting to get the picture here? Very simply, we Americans are starting too late!

Save $1-a-day from age zero to eighteen = $6,570 total saved OR you could do this:

Save $9,768 per year, or $814 per month, from age forty to seventy—for thirty-continuous YEARS!

EITHER CHOICE GETS YOU $1,331,787!

$1-a-day for eighteen years, OR $814 per month for thirty years.

Each account would hypothetically earn the exact same amount of money. Which one would you choose if you saw both options side by side for the very first time?

Start at Age 18	Amount Invested	Total Value	Start at Age 40	Amount Invested	Total Value
Year 1	365	$365	Year 1	0	$0
Year 5	1,825	$2,184	Year 5	0	$0
Year 10	3,650	$5,545	Year 10	0	$0
Year 18	6,570	$15,075	Year 18	0	$0
Year 20	0	$17,911	Year 20	0	$0
Year 25	0	$27,558	Year 25	0	$0
Year 30	0	$42,401	Year 30	0	$0
Year 35	0	$65,239	Year 35	0	$0
Year 40	0	$100,378	Year 40	9,770	$9,770
Year 45	0	$154,445	Year 45	48,852	$58,473
Year 50	0	$237,632	Year 50	97,704	$148,441
Year 55	0	$365,626	Year 55	146,556	$286,868
Year 60	0	$562,561	Year 60	195,408	$499,855
Year 65	0	$865,570	Year 65	244,260	$827,562
Year 70	0	$1,331,787	Year 70	293,112	$1,331,779

Final Amount Earned for each account:
$1,331,779

Total Invested Ages 1-18: **$6,570**

Total Invested Ages 40-70: **$293,112**

Call your financial advisor or CPA right away. Ask them their thoughts on **retirement planning for babies** and what they might recommend.

When is the best time to plant a tree? The answer: twenty years ago. What is the second best time to plant a tree? The answer: right now! So, are you ready to get started? Does the financial plan for the newborn baby require perfection? Answer: no. It requires application. It requires diligence. It requires a decision somebody sticks to for eighteen years. Are you ready to make a decision over the next fifteen to twenty or thirty years that will benefit you similarly?

> **Success principle: True success generally occurs over time. If you have the lottery mentality, the get-rich-quick mentality, or the panic mentality, success may be elusive for you. Remember the tortoise and hare!**

Economic Engine Explained
Your Economic Engine May Be Sputtering Out of Fuel

The day you are born—perhaps even sometimes before—your personal *"Economic Engine"* roars to life. In fact, it is your parents who pour fuel (money) into your economic engine from the first days onward. Sometimes, during the teenage years, your economic engine can receive a "Turbo Boost" with income earned as a teenager. With both parental support AND childhood income, your economic engine begins to rev at full throttle.

Often, during college, our economic engine is running at full capacity, and our parents, in their best *Star Trek* "Scotty voice" will shout, "I am giving it all I've got, Captain; I can't keep her together much longer!" *Whew!* That was a close call. If we played our cards right, we are able to use the Economic Engine provided for by our parents, and embark on the process of creating and fueling our own engines.

Ahhh, now you enjoy that full independence you were so eager to achieve. YOU ARE ON YOUR OWN! Your personal Economic Engine has possibly slowed down a bit as you progress through life and acquire your first "Real Job." The Economic Engine is now under your full power and control. (Oh, and it is just fine now to stay up late on school nights, eat ice cream for breakfast, and drink directly from the milk carton…you are on your own!)

This job may often lead to other jobs. These careers may lead to other careers and opportunity. The average person switches jobs many times during a full lifetime cycle. And often, these jobs offer benefit plans and other opportunities to save for the future. While we will talk about these types of investment programs in later chapters, it is important to know that these savings during your working years, also called "*The Accumulation Phase*" will be the fuel for your future Economic Engine called *Retirement*. Retirement is also called "*The Income Phase*." Be sure you put in the right kind and amount of fuel just in case your Economic Engine needs to run for thirty-fifty years **AFTER your retirement date!**

The Mars Rover is an automated vehicle that propels when initiated. It is designed to last for many years and adjusts to weather conditions.

Your economic engine must operate like a Mars Rover.

At the end of life, your Economic Engine must remain running for those you leave behind, and they need enough fuel to cover the "*Distribution Phase*" of life.

Quick Economics Lesson: There are three stages of your adult economic life:

Life Phases

Accumulation	Income	Distribution

Save money for the future	Spend money in the now	Pass money to spouse, children, charity, IRS

1. Accumulation   Saving money for the future
2. Income   Spending money in the now
3. Distribution   Passing my money to my spouse, children, church, IRS, etc.

Here is another great question to answer:

> **If today an event happened by choice or accident,
> how long could you survive on the amount of money
> you currently have saved?**

Once again, these types of questions, while difficult to face, are the very questions you WILL face when your traditional economic engine (job) comes to an end. Let's get to work answering these questions, finding REAL solutions, and taking the right steps to secure our financial futures. This country is too great to have so many families suffering financially. But let me offer up an idea:

YOU <u>CAN</u> FIX IT.

YOU <u>WILL</u> FIX IT.

THE GOVERNMENT WILL
<u>NEVER</u> FIX IT FOR YOU.

YOU WILL <u>BE GLAD</u> YOU FIXED IT.

Chapter Two
Taking Immediate Action Regardless of Your Current Financial Condition

Rule: Waiting might save you money, but it costs you time. You can get more money, but you cannot get more time. Take action now

My dad, Charles, is the ultimate jokester. Back in the early 60s, my sweet old pops thought it would be just hilarious to name his two boys something funny. Our first possible name choice would have paid respects to our uncles Mortimer and Eggbert. I would have been "Eggie," and my brother would have been "Morty." Fate intervened. Given my dad's position as a grocery-store clerk at Thurman's Cash and Carry Grocery, I became Cash and my brother was to become Carey. Cash and Carey. Funny stuff when you are in the first grade in a small town. EVERYONE was in on the joke!

My brother is one of my heroes, and I always took every opportunity to follow him around, copy him, or collaborate with him on big things. In the '70s we started Cash and Carey's Lawn Improvement Service. Our first business together! We did so many things together and I cherish those times. For the rest of our time here in this book, I will share an occasional story of two brothers, Cash and Carey, whose paths, although similar, turned out quite different. In each of the stories, one of the brothers took one path, one took the other path. These stories will illuminate certain financial concepts and from them, you will gain valuable insight. (Sorry Carey—you are so brilliant in real life, I had to change the characters and make you the goof in these stories!)

Cash and Carey Buy a Car

I enjoy a nice cultural phenomenon. One such phenomenon occurs during a moment when a young man or woman reaches one of those major life goals called college graduation. Inevitably, the newly-crowned graduate breaks out into the world, is fully on his/her own, has his/her first real job, and is ready to begin life. For many, that first major expense is usually (in my game-show-announcer voice) **a brand-new car!**

While the world enjoys the sweet smell of success and almost every person on the planet enjoys the sweet smell of a brand-new car, we ought to be equating that car with the sweet smell of the first big mistake many of us make. Let me illustrate a story that I think you'll really enjoy. Well, "enjoy" may not be the right word; this is a story that I hope will wake you up to something that millions of people do every year and have no idea how it impacts them long-term.

Carey buys a nice car immediately after graduating from college. Despite having student loans, Carey purchases a new truck for $42,500 and pays $2,500 down. His payments over a sixty-month period—assuming a 4% interest rate—would be $736.66 monthly. Cool! Carey gets his dream truck!

Cash decides to drive his old beater car. You know the one with occasional problems, and smokes like crazy. Cash decides to SAVE that same $736.66 monthly that Carey is spending for five years in a savings account earning just 4% per year. No, an additional $736.66 did not just show up. Cash just acts like he has a payment, and chooses to put that money into a savings account. At the end of the five years, Cash will have $47,879 in REAL CASH MONEY. To be fair, his car is awful, but his bank account is amazing! He is now twenty-six years old with a nice nest egg saved for his future.

From THAT point, Cash invests the $47,879 he saved and earns 9% per year. (See disclaimer) How much would that same $47,879 grow to at his projected retirement age of 70? Answer? $2,122,809. WOW! It is amazing how just one decision early in life can positively or negatively affect your outcome. Are you currently living with the impact and results of decisions made long ago?

Cash DIDN'T buy a new car and saved that money for just five years, then deposited **that** money and earned an extra $2,122,809.

Hmmm. This is a new kind of price-sticker shock. Carey: "*I don't want to talk about it.*"

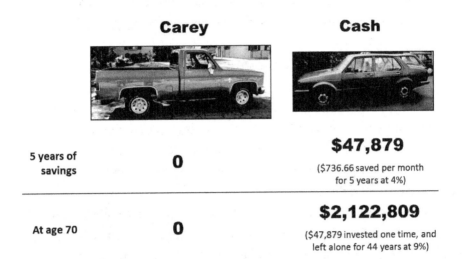

	Carey	Cash
5 years of savings	**0**	**$47,879** ($736.66 saved per month for 5 years at 4%)
At age 70	**0**	**$2,122,809** ($47,879 invested one time, and left alone for 44 years at 9%)

The Reality of Bad Financial Judgment

Wisdom is something usually learned AFTER making a mistake. We rarely learn from doing something right. For me, in the example above, I learned that making just one "normal" decision could make ALL the difference at my retirement. So, if the rest of the crowd is doing it, most likely, it is a BAD idea!

Here is some reality to flavor the rest of this chapter:

- If you are forty years old, and plan to retire at age sixty-five, AND you get paid once a month, you have 300 paychecks left in your lifetime before you have to live on the value of your savings!
- The average fifty-four-year-old man has about $20,000 in total cash savings. He has just 132 pay periods left to get it right.
- The average American-taxpaying family voluntarily overpays their income taxes an average of $3,000 per year. While "famous" tax preparation companies glorify this behavior, isn't it silly to overpay a bill that simply is NOT due!?

- If seventy-year-old you could come back in time and talk to you today, what would you tell yourself to do financially, <u>RIGHT NOW?</u>

Getting Started Now

Getting started is simply a decision. Have you made that type of decision for you and your family? What are you waiting for? Do you need someone else's approval BEFORE you allow yourself to be a success? You don't need money to get started. You don't need much of an education to get started the RIGHT way and right AWAY.

All you need is a clear vision of what you want, and a realistic game plan to get you there! Sounds simple, right? That's because it is EASY to make a decision. Good decisions are FREE, but worth EVERYTHING!

Perhaps the best way I know to get started is to seek advice from someone who either has what you want or knows how to get there. You may want to talk to your spouse, your financial advisor, a banker, or a CPA. The important thing is to sit down with someone, put your heads together, and GET STARTED ON THE PLAN!

That is it . . . decide to decide.

A friend of mine was telling me his story about how he stopped smoking. He didn't *stop* smoking on a particular day; he *decided* to stop smoking on a particular day. He then set out on a course of action that, just sixty days later, helped him stop smoking forever. You can decide, <u>right now</u>, to change and improve your financial life.

Decide to Decide

- Make an honest appraisal of your financial life
- If you are married, or have a significant other, include your person in your journey

Set a timeframe that you will begin correcting problems or attaining goals. After seeking wise counsel, consulting with your person, and determining your next course of action, it is vital that you get started right away. The cost of waiting is simply too high!

Create a budget with yourself and your person. Put everything on it. Nothing spared. Look at your paycheck. Examine your bank statements. Are there things listed in your paycheck or your bank statement that you don't understand—all of which cost you money? Are there gym memberships that you never use? Examine every single item that you spend money on and let's make a preliminary list of what we can cut or improve. Make a commitment not to be emotionally attached to the outcome. There is no blame in this step. Take it easy on yourself while being tough on yourself!

We will talk a little later what to do with this budget, but the first important thing is to understand where your money goes. Make sure to give yourself enough quality time with your bills and expenses so that you don't get hurried or stop the project before it is finished. The planning stage of anything excellent should take a substantial amount of time. This will be one of the greatest investments you ever make in your financial life.

After you have your list, begin to examine all of your expenses. For example, are you using that gym membership? Have you compared prices on your auto insurance? Do you have other insurance drafts coming out of your paycheck or checking account and you have no idea what they go to? Do you have multiple insurance policies where you could consolidate down to one and not lose any benefit?

Have you called your cell-phone company to see if there's a better rate available? Are you getting a tax refund? Did you know you can call your HR department tomorrow and reduce the amount of money you're having taken out of your paycheck? If you're not sure how to do this, check with your CPA or financial advisor. They could be able to coach you. How much cable TV do you watch? Is there a cheaper plan that you could switch to and still have most of the entertainment value? Would Netflix be a better option for you and your family right now?

I am not proposing a life of full austerity. I am proposing a life of ***controlled prosperity***. You deserve it. As you can see, it takes work! And there is only one place where success comes BEFORE work...and that is the dictionary! Be prepared to put in some work here. *Controlled Prosperity* equals **Freedom with Responsibility**.

FME:
Frequently Made Excuses for Not Starting

1. I don't have the time

2. I don't know what to do, or how to do it—money is confusing

3. I will let my spouse do it

4. It is a waste of time; I am too smart to start with small amounts of money; twenty bucks here and there won't make a difference; I don't have enough money to invest; I'm living month-to-month

5. I will wait until I have thousands to invest or until I have thousands to pay off this debt before I set forth on a serious plan

6. Everyone's in this condition; what difference does it make if I'm not financially fit?

Why It Is Important to Get Started Now

Look at the difference between Column A and Column B. Two people of identical age are saving money for the future:

The High Cost of Waiting

Person A

- Starts at age 25
- Saves $2000 a year for 10 years (ages 25-35)
- Invests a total of $20,000

Person B

- Starts at age 35 (10 years later)
- Saves $2000 a year for 30 years (ages 35-65)
- Invests a total of $60,000

Age	Amount Invested	Total Value	Age	Amount Invested	Total Value
25	2000.00	2160.00	25	0.00	0.00
26	2000.00	4492.80	26	0.00	0.00
27	2000.00	7012.22	27	0.00	0.00
28	2000.00	9733.20	28	0.00	0.00
29	2000.00	12671.86	29	0.00	0.00
30	2000.00	15845.61	30	0.00	0.00
31	2000.00	19273.26	31	0.00	0.00
32	2000.00	22975.12	32	0.00	0.00
33	2000.00	26973.12	33	0.00	0.00
34	2000.00	31290.97	34	0.00	0.00
35	0.00	33794.25	35	2000.00	2160.00
36	0.00	36497.79	36	2000.00	4492.8
37	0.00	39417.62	37	2000.00	7012.22
38	0.00	42571.03	38	2000.00	9733.20
39	0.00	45976.71	39	2000.00	12671.86
40	0.00	49654.84	40	2000.00	15845.61
41	0.00	53627.23	41	2000.00	19273.26
42	0.00	57917.41	42	2000.00	22975.12
43	0.00	62550.80	43	2000.00	26973.12
44	0.00	67554.87	44	2000.00	31290.97
45	0.00	72959.26	45	2000.00	35954.25
46	0.00	78796.00	46	2000.00	40990.59
47	0.00	85099.68	47	2000.00	46429.84
48	0.00	91907.65	48	2000.00	52304.23
49	0.00	99260.26	49	2000.00	58648.57
so	0.00	107201.09	50	2000.00	65500.45
51	0.00	115777.17	51	2000.00	72900.49
52	0.00	125039.35	52	2000.00	80892.53
53	0.00	135042.49	53	2000.00	89523.93
54	0.00	145845.89	54	2000.00	98845.84
55	0.00	157513.56	55	2000.00	108913.51
56	0.00	170114.65	56	2000.00	119786.59
57	0.00	183723.82	57	2000.00	131529.52
58	0.00	198421.73	58	2000.00	144211.88
59	0.00	214295.47	59	2000.00	157908.83
60	0.00	231439.10	60	2000.00	172701.54
61	0.00	249954.23	61	2000.00	188677.66
62	0.00	269950.57	62	2000.00	205931.87
63	0.00	291546.62	63	2000.00	224566.42
64	0.00	314870 .34	64	2000.00	244691.74
65	0.00	340059.97	65	2000.00	266427.07
	$20,000	$340,059		$60,000	$266,427

Investment Difference:

Person A invested this much less than Person B:

$40,000

Results Difference:

Person A ended up with this much **more** than Person B:

$73,632

Person A started investing at age twenty-five, then quit at age thirty-five and left the money invested until age sixty-five. Person B WAITED ten years, then began to save from age thirty-five until sixty-five, a total of thirty years! What one person accomplished in ten years, took the other nearly thirty years to accomplish. Think about that!

Right now you are saying, *"Cash, I wish I knew this at 25. I would have behaved differently. But I'm not, so I am going to stay the way I am."* If you do nothing, then I have failed as an author. Waiting at ANY age costs you.

Let's take a fifty-year-old who has $20,000 to his name. He wants to retire at age sixty-five. He makes $70,000 per year. What if he starts saving 30% of his annual income right now? 30% is hard, but he is behind, so he needs to do something drastic. Let's see how much he might have at age sixty-five.

> **30% of $70,000 or $21,000 saved each year for fifteen years, which earns 9% = $616,579 at age sixty-five.**

"That sounds good, Cash! But 30% is a lot. And things are tight right now. I'm going to save that money and start this plan as soon as I get my ducks in a row. I am going to wait a year to get started." How does **waiting one year until age fifty-one** impact you?

> **30% of 70,000 or 21,000 saved each year for fourteen years, which earns 9% = $546,403 at age sixty-five.**

You "saved" $21,000, but LOST the potential value of $70,176.

Perhaps you wait five more years. Waiting five years costs another $297,528. No matter what your age, it is critical that you act RIGHT NOW.

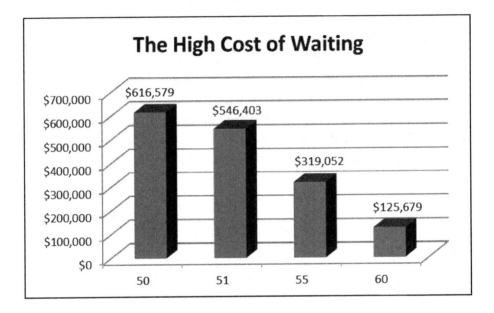

The values on the chart above reflect approximate values achieved by investing over time, assuming different starting points. (Age fifty, Age fifty-one, etc.) and ending at age sixty-five. The high-cost-of-waiting example is screaming for you to get started now!

Too many people wait for the "perfect time" to get started. There is no perfect time to do something great for yourself. Right now IS the perfect time!

Getting started requires YOU to take the first step. It sort of goes like this when you want to accomplish something:

1. A thought occurs to do something specific; this leads to personal contemplation, also called, "Thinking about it," or in Oklahoma-slang, "I am fixin-to"
2. Personal contemplation (thinking about it) leads to a decision
3. Decisions lead to actions. Ready! Aim! Fire! Some of you will go, "Fire! Aim! Ready? Retreat!"
4. Plan, Do, Review; best advice ever. Make the plan, work the plan, review the plan, repeat if necessary

So, follow your own yellow-brick road! You have the desires of your financial heart identified. You can see the destination somewhere in the future. You have courage to get started. And just like in the greatest movie ever, *The Wizard of Oz*, you may find a few hazards along the way. Don't fret. I've watched this financial movie in advance for you, and I can tell you it is going to be all right! I don't want to spoil the ending, but it IS going to be just fine . . . IF you get started, and IF you avoid the flesh-eating flying monkeys (procrastination, taxes, etc.). Enjoy the rest of your movie.

Chapter Three
Avoid These Four Financial Disasters

The Four Dreaded Horsemen
of Your Financial Future

Rule: Bad things happen when you don't pay attention. So, pay attention!

These are the flesh-eating flying monkeys I warned you about.

I realize that it's difficult reading through the first two chapters, because it stirred up a of lot feelings—mainly that things are not going okay. I want to take a moment and address the feelings some of you may be having. I share these things with you so that you can take stock and get an accurate appraisal of your own financial life. They are <u>NOT</u> meant to scare you or worry you. Rather, they <u>are</u> meant to cause you to take <u>swift and immediate action</u>.

Isn't it a great thing that we live in a country where we can virtually start over almost every day? In many parts of the world, that freedom doesn't exist. Right here in the USA, regardless of your status, regardless of the amount of time you have left, regardless of your past, regardless of your education, you are allowed to start over every single day!

TAKE A MOMENT RIGHT NOW AND COUNT YOUR BLESSINGS THAT YOU LIVE IN THE USA OR OTHER FREE COUNTRY WHERE YOU CAN ACTUALLY START OVER EVERY DAY!

If you lived in Haiti, or some communist country, your rights and abilities to start over might be limited. Your geography here allows you to become anything you want to be and to erase any wrong as long as you're willing to put out the effort. So that is my question for you at this point: Are you really willing to put out the effort to succeed? When? Something I learned a long time ago is that no one is going to hand you financial success. But financial success leaves clues, and throughout this book I want to share those clues with you. Financial failure also leaves clues. In this chapter, we examine four of the main *financial roadblocks* faced by almost every American citizen. We call them the ***Four Dreaded Horsemen of Your Financial Future***. Sounds ominous, right? **It is**.

By analyzing these four common areas, we can be prepared for the coming wave of financial challenges. It is important to be aware of speed bumps in your path. The four areas we are about to discuss here are more than speed bumps. In fact, they are speed traps. They affect almost every person equally—whether you're rich or poor. Knowing and preparing for these four silent killers will set you ahead financially, and give you the enduring financial peace you desire.

The old saying goes that time is on your side. I disagree! Time is not on your side. In fact, time is slipping away. However, if you can remember the acronym T.I.M.E. you can better prepare for what lies in your financial future.

T. I. M. E.

The *T* in T.I.M.E. stands for *Taxes*. Taxes are the first "Deadly Horseman" of your financial future. There are some interesting facts about taxes that I think you should understand. You will work from January 1 through May 1 just to pay your income taxes. 15% of every dollar that you have earned has been paid into the Social Security system. Do you count this as a tax? I do! 86% of American taxpayers do their taxes wrong and overpay their taxes an average of $3,000 per year. 86%! Why on earth would we ever pay a bill that isn't due? Finally, how big will the tax bill on your 401(k) or IRA be during retirement? There are multitudes of ways to get the tax thing WRONG. CONSIDER THIS:

PUT THE WORD "THE" AND "IRS" TOGETHER....
WHAT DOES IT SPELL?
THEIRS!

If you consider the overall nature of your financial life, I believe that taxes have been and will always be your single largest bill. How you choose to prepare your taxes is up to you. The Supreme Court has ruled that an individual has the right to arrange their taxes in such a way so as to pay as little tax as possible. It doesn't make you patriotic to overpay your taxes. Simply put, it makes you broke!

How then are we to deal with this touchy subject of taxes? People fear the IRS; they fear underpaying their taxes—which very few do. In my experience, the IRS is actually a quite pleasant group to work with. They are just out to collect what is owed, and not a penny more. If you ever have questions for the IRS, it's a great idea to include your CPA in those conversations as they speak the IRS language. The biggest problems I see aren't those problems inflicted upon our citizens. Nope! The biggest problems I see in the world of taxes are those problems that we volunteer, that we sign up for, and that we bring unto ourselves!

Is your IRA an IOU to the IRS?

To top all of this off, the Social Security payments that you receive during retirement may now also be subject to the federal income tax! Back in the 1930s when Social Security was introduced as 'The Old Age Savings Plan," it was itself a tax on individual earnings. It was **never** meant to be taxed as income in any way.

For millions of individuals and families who get Social Security, it is now included in the calculations for income on your annual tax return! Unfortunately, "tax reform" brought new taxes on Social Security payments. Shocking! Does this bother you? I didn't think it was supposed to be this way. For roughly 75% of the American population over sixty-five, Social Security supplies the majority of their retirement income. And for some, these payments may now be subject to the federal income tax! It is your responsibility to understand when and where taxes apply and what YOU can do to avoid them.

Are there ways we can legally *__avoid overpaying income tax__*? ABSOLUTELY!

There is a major difference between tax preparation and tax planning.

1. **Immediately stop *__overpaying__* your personal income taxes**. Call your HR department today if you're getting a tax refund and make the correct adjustment to your exemptions so that your tax bill actually matches what is owed. Talk to your tax person to figure out how to accomplish this. You do not want to UNDERPAY your taxes either, but overpaying them is the wrong approach

2. **Maximize deductions**. It is my opinion that you should work with a qualified tax advisor or CPA when doing your taxes; they know how to take advantage of all the legal deductions and keep you out of trouble; interview several tax professionals and work closely with your tax person as you grow your financial life; they can help steer you and put you put you on the right track

3. **Use the right business entity**. If you run a small business or earn income on the side, make sure you have the right kind of business entity set up; different entities are taxed at different rates, and some may have different exclusions; for example, an LLC or a corporation may have a different, more favorable tax structure than being independently self-employed or a sole proprietor; ask your tax professional which of these entities is perfect for your situation; you will be glad you did

4. **Analyze an IRA to a Roth conversion**. Consider the effects of taxation during retirement; would it make economic sense to convert your traditional IRA, 401(k), etc., to the tax-free Roth IRA? Normally, IRA distributions are fully taxable and may also cause your Social Security to

become taxable; would it make sense for you to investigate the feasibility of converting your current IRA-type accounts into the more tax-favorable Roth accounts?

5. **Imagine the answer to this question if you were a farmer**: would you rather pay income taxes on your seeds or your crops? Think about that for a moment! When we choose an IRA, we essentially sign up to pay the tax on the full value of our grown crops. Might there be a better way? This is one math equation worth learning!

Just for "fun," here is a list of *potential* taxes you pay just by being an American:

1. Accounts Receivable Tax
2. Building Permit Tax
3. Capital Gains Tax
4. CDL License Tax
5. Cigarette Tax
6. Corporate Income Tax
7. Court Fines
8. Dog License Tax
9. Federal Income Tax
10. Federal Unemployment Tax (FUTA)
11. Fishing License Tax
12. Food License Tax
13. Fuel Permit Tax
14. Gasoline Tax
15. Hunting License Tax
16. Inheritance Tax
17. Interest Expense
18. Inventory Tax
19. IRS Interest Charges
20. IRS Penalties
21. Liquor Tax

22. Local Income Tax
23. Luxury Taxes
24. Marriage License Tax
25. Medicare Tax
26. Property Tax
27. Real Estate Tax
28. Recreational Vehicle Tax
29. Road Toll Booth Taxes
30. Road Usage Taxes (truckers)
31. Sales Taxes
32. School Tax
33. Septic Permit Tax
34. Service Charge Taxes
35. Social Security Tax
36. State Income Tax
37. State Unemployment Tax (SUTA)
38. Telephone Federal Excise Tax
39. Telephone Federal, State and Local Surcharge Taxes
40. Telephone Federal Universal Service Fee Tax
41. Telephone Minimum Usage Surcharge Tax
42. Telephone Recurring and Nonrecurring Charges Tax
43. Telephone State and Local Tax
44. Telephone Usage Charge Tax
45. Toll Bridge Taxes Toll
46. Tunnel Taxes
47. Trailer Registration
48. Tax Utility Taxes
49. Vehicle License Registration Tax
50. Vehicle Sales Tax
51. Watercraft Registration Tax
52. Well Permit Tax

How far into each year do you have to go before you have worked enough to pay your federal income taxes? Today, **all** of the money we make between January 1 and May 1 goes just to pay our income taxes!

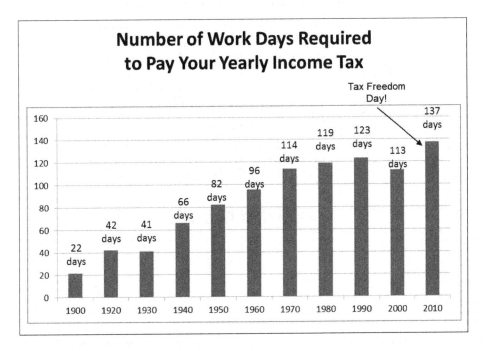

Number of Work Days Required to Pay Your Yearly Income Tax

T. I. M. E.

The *I* in T.I.M.E. stands for *Inflation*. Inflation is the second Deadly Horseman of your financial plan. This is one of the true silent-but-deadly issues we deal with on an ongoing basis.

Simply put, prices are going up. Will your income keep up with the average price increases going on in the world? There are many kinds of inflation. The government reports the CPI, or The Consumer Price Index, as one measure of economic activity and inflation. Over long periods of time, the government has reported that the overall inflation rate has been around 3 to 4%. But I would ask you to consider what is called *"personal inflation."* Personal inflation is inflation on smaller daily expenditure-type items like milk and medicine and gasoline. How much has the price of gasoline risen in the last couple years?

In fact, the price has almost tripled in some areas. How has your personal-inflation rate been affecting you?

Price of daily purchases

	Gallon of Gas	Postage Stamp	Eggs	Gallon of Milk
1942	19¢	3¢	38¢	60¢
1960	31¢	4¢	57¢	49¢
1978	63¢	15¢	82¢	$1.71
1996	$1.23	32¢	$1.31	$3.30
2014	$2.95	49¢	$1.69	$3.67

Speed of Growth

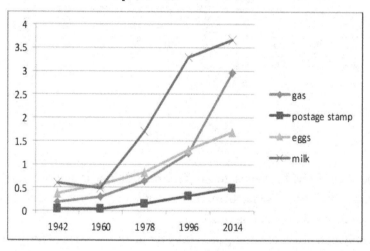

Here's an interesting fact: let's assume that inflation is 4% per year for the next eighteen years. What this really means to you is that over the next eighteen years the basic prices of things will double based on the inflation rate. To put this in better perspective, it would equally require that you double your income during the next eighteen years or learn to live on half of what you live on now! Think about that for a moment: learn to live on half.

> **If inflation continues at 4% per year for the next eighteen years, you will have to double your income, or learn to live on half!**

My Dad's Story

Growing up in a small town seems like an ideal life. In the early days, my father worked for the grocery store as a sack boy and managed to start his family on just a $200-a-month worth of income. And while things were very tight, somehow, we survived.

Sometime in the mid-60s my dad was offered a job with the Rock Island Railroad. This job, while much harder, also offered the availability of benefits, like a retirement-pension fund. It also came with a substantial wage increase where my dad was making approximately $500 a month. Now when you're used to earning $200 a month and you get a job making $500 a month, and it has a retirement pension to boot, it's easy to lure yourself to sleep thinking that you have it made.

Now if you could, just for a moment, put on your 1968 glasses and imagine going from $200 a month, to earning $500 a month, and then have your employer promise you a _lifetime pension of $1000 a month_! That's right, a promise of $1,000 a month once you reach age 65. To a previously-poor family, the thought of making $1,000 a month, *someday*, seemed wildly wonderful! Now, take off your 1968 glasses and imagine what my dad's life might be like in 2015 once his railroad retirement pension came to life. Someday is today, and $1,000 is not enough money.

In this modern era with modest inflation, my father is now forced to live the rest of his life on just $1,000 a month. What did the railroad pension forget to include? Inflation! That's right; a simple 3 to 4% inflation rate rendered what seemed to be an amazing retirement absolutely unlivable just 40 years later.

My father was not a bad guy; in fact, he's a very good man. He is smart, articulate, and generous. But unfortunately, he was not prepared to deal with the negative impacts of inflation. They don't teach this in high school. They don't teach this in college, either! If you fail to learn and deal with inflation, you might get the same type of results. Consider how vast your own lifetime might be.

Contemplate how long you will need your money to work diligently for you. Imagine what it might be like to retire at sixty-five, then live to age 100! You would have to live off your savings and retirement plan for thirty-five continuous years!

Inflation is a type of financial cancer, and it has very few symptoms. It just sneaks up on you. And before you know it, what once was a great retirement is now a paltry existence. Wealthy people understand and take precautions in regard to inflation. How will you deal with this nefarious problem? **The *I* in the acronym T.I.M.E. stands for inflation; remember, the *T* stood for taxes.**

> **Consider this example: Robert is thirty-five years old, and earns $70,000 per year. At age seventy-one, he will need $287,275 per year walking in the door, every year, to live a comparable lifestyle like he did at age thirty-five. Why? Inflation. If inflation runs at 4% per year, he will need to DOUBLE HIS INCOME EVERY EIGHTEEN YEARS!**

Important question for you and your spouse:

> **If inflation is 4% a year between today and the time you turn sixty-five, how much money will you need walking in the door at age sixty-five to successfully retire?**

T.I.M.E

The *M* in T.I.M.E stands for the *Market*. The third Deadly Horseman of your financial life is the market. Here, we discuss the potential negative impact of the market. The stock market has been around over 100 years, and at various times is either rising, falling or staying flat. It is always exciting to go to a party when people ask, *"Cash, what do you think the market is going to do?"* I usually say something brilliant like, *"Well, the market might go up, or it might go down, and it is quite possible that it will just sit there for a while and not do much at all."*

In the late 1970s and early 1980s, prior to the onslaught of the internet and the gradual switch over to the 401(k), very few investors were actually in the stock market. But by the mid-to-late 1990s, nearly 80% of the families in America had some type of exposure to the market. Usually, this exposure was in the form of a 401(k), IRA, Roth IRA, or 403(b).

These were amazing times. The tech bubble was among us upon us in the late '90s and it seemed like all you had to do was be in the market to win. You didn't need a lot of knowledge and you had a great chance to make a lot of money for yourself. Unfortunately, many of these investors were new to the concept of investing. It seemed like a free-for-all at the candy store, when in fact, the up-and-down side of the market was still in play.

From the year 2000 to 2008 the market endured significant losses of investor principle. Without going into individual stocks or specific fund investments, we can use the US Standard and Poor 500 Index to measure certain types of market volatility. In fact, if we measure the cumulative losses of 2000, 2001, 2002, and then again in 2008 and part of 2009, the market fell nearly 85%! ***How well are you going to do financially when you give back 85% of—not just your profits, but your principle as well?*** Even after a smaller downturn of 10% or 15% or 20%, how long does it take for the market to correct itself to the upside?

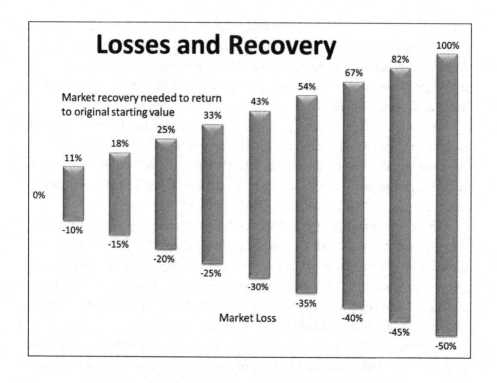

"The Roll-In Period"

I consider the seven to ten years just prior to your proposed retirement date as the most significant period of your investment life. It is during these times that even a modest downturn in the market might have a significant economic impact on your long-term financial life. A sudden downturn could prolong your working years significantly. The OBJECTIVE is not to **get** retired; it is to **stay** retired! What would happen to you if your life savings decreased 20% in just one year through no fault of your own? And when you're taking money from your retirement account alongside a declining market, the impact could be even more devastating. How can we make it up? For most, the answer is *never*. This could be an irreversible mistake.

And after analyzing the previous chart on recovery times, I believe it is much more important for somebody within ten years of retirement to have an extra level of modesty in their investing strategy.

Consider this example: if you earn 50% in one year, then lose 50% in the next year, how have you done? Many believe that you have broken even. Let's do it in longhand math and check your answer.

Start with $100,000

Earn 50% to the principle:
$100,000 + 50% = $150,000

Now, lose 50%!
$150,000 − 50% = $75,000.

Gaining 50% then Losing 50% adds up to MINUS 25%

Remember the three phases of your financial life? There might be a fourth phase!

1. Accumulation (Time to save)

2. Income (Time to spend)

3. Distribution (Time to pass money on)

4. Desperation (Time to panic!) You may not feel, or realize, that you are actively in any of the "Three Phases." While the "*Desperation Phase*" is not actually part of the three phases, it is a phase that I see in play quite often. If you are in the *Desperation Phase*, seek help immediately!

Too many people in the desperation phase take too many unnecessary risks during the roll-in period. During this last part of the "accumulation phase," it is vital that you protect your savings and retirement accounts from market losses.

> **To keep your retirement plan Rollin', you must be careful during the Roll In!**

Risk

When we think of risk, we usually think about the stock market going down. Are there other kinds of risk? The answer is a resounding YES! Not only is a falling market a type of risk, we should consider all of these other risks as well:

- Inflation, as stated above
- Market going up and we aren't in it at all
- Death or disability
- Aging parents who live with us
- Older children who fail to launch
- Taxes…always taking a steady big bite

A risk is ANYTHING that makes our values less. Does the list above pose a threat of any kind to YOUR financial world? If so, we must plan for these items in advance. (That might mean giving your kids their "grow up" speech sooner rather than later!) Risk comes in many forms, NOT just from the stock market!

The *E* in T.I.M.E stands for *Emergencies.* The fourth Deadly Horseman of your financial life is unplanned economic emergencies. What constitutes an emergency? Certainly the day-to-day frustrations of a flat tire or a broken refrigerator always hit us at an inconvenient time. Almost every emergency has a price tag with it. Generally, later in life, these types of emergencies are less important than the bigger ones we might encounter. For this conversation, let's just have an agreement that somewhere in our life, we will have a few thousand dollars in our emergency fund for the day-to-day emergencies and that we need to take better and more calculated steps to deal with the larger *life-changing emergencies.*

THESE Emergencies
Can Shut Down Your Economic Engine!

- **Disability**. If your income stopped today through no fault or choice of your own, how long could you live on your savings?
- **Medical care**. Do you have sufficient reserves to meet deductibles, extended hospital stays, assisted-living requirements, or other medical emergencies? One in four people spends the last two years of their life in some type of long-term care facility. If this happened to you or a loved one, how would this affect your financial life?
- **Unexpected death of a spouse or family member**. Are you adequately prepared for the unthinkable? Would the loss of one of your Social Security checks set you back? Does your pension have spousal continuation benefits? Do you have ample "nearby cash reserves" or adequate insurance for these contingencies?
- **Elderly parents for whom we take responsibility**. With life expectancy increasing, what would it look like if you became the primary care giver for an elderly parent or relative?
- **Adult children with financial needs**. Are your children independent of you? Have they somehow been your economic priority? What is the right way to deal with your adult children?
- **Increasing taxes of many kinds**. With social security being taxable now, and IRA distributions being fully taxable, are you prepared to deal with income taxes, property taxes, taxes on Social Security, estate taxes, or gift taxes?
- **Last minute loss of job**. The cleanest of plans is no match for the mess of reality. Many of us have plans to work until a certain age, or we plan to exit the job market at a certain level of savings. What happens if your employer has a different idea than that? Are you prepared for the unexpected loss of fuel prior to crossing the finish line?

Talking about these things is really just depressing. Right? It is equally depressing to actually endure these things without having an economic plan to deal with them. Unfortunately, I am not just talking theoretically. I see it with clients every day. Let's agree to discuss these potential emergencies, address them, then create and **implement** a plan to deal with the ravages of an unplanned financial life. You wouldn't get in your car for a long-distance trip without some kind of map. Let's make a few adjustments to your economic road map. Your economic engine will be fine with the right kind of tune up. You will too!

T.I.M.E. = Taxes, Inflation, Markets, Emergencies

We have this tendency as people to blame ourselves more than necessary. The fact is, taxes, inflation, market issues, and emergencies are NOT your fault in any way. You can take a breath here and recognize that life is tough sometimes. Here is perhaps the best lesson I learned as a young person when my own life was not turning out the way I had wished for:

> **AT THE EXACT MOMENT YOU REALIZE THAT LIFE
> IS HARD, LIFE BECOMES EASY!**

Some of you blame yourselves for the events listed in T.I.M.E.; I want you to know that it isn't your entire fault. However, it is your responsibility to take steps from right here, right where you are.

Give it all you can as long as you can. Winners run THROUGH the finish line, not TO the finish line. Accept the difficult nature of life, and it becomes a beautiful yet challenging experiment!

In the next chapter, we will talk about the menu choices available for you and begin the process of developing your own program.

Don't stop now. Starting is easy. Finishing well is where you win the trophy! Let's get ready to get ready!

Chapter Four
Financial Constipation:
Is Your Economic Engine Out of Gas?

Rule: Your regular way of financial planning may leave you feeling a bit irregular

You may want to grab a cup of coffee right about now. In this chapter, we will discuss the **many** programs and concepts available to the typical American family. There are literally thousands of ways to save and invest money in the United States. If you have been around the investing and financial markets long enough, you have seen a multitude of investment strategies come and go.

In the early '80s, when I entered the financial market as an advisor, the options were much more limited for the basic investor. The IRA and the 401(k) were relatively new to the marketplace. The internet had not yet taken hold. Corporations were more likely to provide you a lifetime pension than they were a 401(k) plan. The availability of quality financial information was very limited to the general public, and usually only available to the wealthy.

That has all changed today. Online trading, thousands of mutual fund offerings, IRA, Roth IRA, 401(k), have all changed the landscape of the financial markets. Corporations—rather than providing pensions—usually provide access to a 401(k) program for its employees. And with government regulation increasing, fewer and fewer employers are offering advanced benefits where they might match your contributions. The marketplace generally shifted from pension funds (defined benefit programs where you knew how much you would get the rest your life), and gradually switched over to defined contribution plans. (Defined contribution generally stipulated that the employee would make the majority of the contributions subject to certain limitations).

Defined Benefit = Pension for Life or Stated Length of Time. Paid for by the ***employer***.

Defined Contribution: Paid by the *employee* with optional employer matching. These have limits on how much can be contributed to retirement plans (401k, SEP, 457, etc.).

Can you see how this shift in thinking may have affected you?

> **While you were sleeping, the entire retirement program that our country relied on for so many decades changed.**

We went from programs that were formerly paid by our employer, to programs that were mostly paid by us, the employee. Today in the United States there are 80 million baby boomers preparing to enter this new retirement realm. ___Almost 10,000 people a day are turning sixty-five___ and this trend will continue for the next twenty years! I wonder if these people are prepared. I wonder if their reliance on their employer to take care retirement has left them in a perilous position. It is time to rethink this thing called retirement.

Here is a basic list of the programs available today for people who like to save money. I will include the most popular forms of investing, saving, and planning. While this list won't cover everything available, it should be a wide enough list to touch on the types of programs you are most likely to see.

The Investment Menu

1. IRA Accounts

2. 401(k) Savings

3. Stocks and Bonds: Market Investments

4. Real Estate

5. Commodities (Gold, Silver, Oil, etc.)

6. Banks, Credit Union Accounts

7. Mutual Funds

Before we begin to dig in to each of these investments, it is only fair that I praise each of them in their own respective way. In fact, each of the above investments used in the correct way, and at the correct time, may represent a fantastic way to get ahead and stay ahead.

Many people have used a variety of investment styles to win the money game. For the purposes of this book, our comments will be generic in nature, and we will not mention a specific stock, fund, or commodity that you ought to invest money in. Instead, we will discuss each of the relevant points that might affect your particular situation.

Before we go into each of these concepts, I want to share certain mathematical formulas with you. These are very easy to understand. The first is called The Rule of 72; the second I simply call +50-50. (We discussed +50/-50 in the last chapter).

The Rule of 72 is a very simple way to estimate how often your money might double at a particular annual interest rate. The calculation is this: whatever interest rate you estimate that you're receiving, divide that number into seventy-two. Let's use a rate of return of 6% annually for our first example. $72 \div 6 = 12$. So, money invested at 6% annually, ought to double every twelve years. Easy, right?

Let's take a look at a really simple graph using The Rule of 72 to understand the compound effect of interest rates on your money. I'm not suggesting that you will earn any of these particular interest rates, but I do think it is important to understand interest rates **and** time on the end result of your money.

Let's take a look at a set of triplets who are twenty-nine years old. Each one has $1,000 to invest. Each one wants to know how much they could have when they retire at age 65. We will use The Rule of 72 to give them their answer. We start by listing the facts: three people, the same age, the exact same amount of money, and the same amount of time. The only difference is the interest rate they might earn on different investment accounts.

Calculating the Speed of Growth
Using the Rule of 72

	Age	6%		Age	12%		Age	18%
		(72 ÷ 6 = 12)			(72 ÷ 12 = 6)			(72 ÷ 18 = 4)
12 years	29	$1,000		29	$1,000		29	$1000
	41	$2,000		35	$2,000		33	$2,000
	53	$4,000		41	$4,000		37	$4,000
	65	$8,000		47	$8,000		41	$8,000
				53	$16,000		45	$16,000
			6 years	59	$32,000		49	$32,000
				65	$64,000		53	$64,000
						4 years	57	$128,000
							61	$256,000
							65	$512,000

The Rule of 72 is a great conversation piece, and a neat way to understand how time and interest may work together.

The second of my examples is called +50-50. I believe this is especially important during the roll-in period as mentioned earlier as you get within ten years of retirement. For the sake of this example, we are going to use both a loss of 50% and a gain of 50% to understand the magnitude of gains and losses. After viewing this graph, you will understand how a significant loss of one number and an equally significant gain of that exact same number doesn't always even the playing field.

> **A Gain of 50% and a Subsequent Loss of 50% Does NOT Have Equal Results on Your Money!**

So what if in one year your accounts grew 50%, and then in the following year they lost 50%? In most worlds +50 and -50 equals zero. It looks like it—at least is a break-even proposition. Not TRUE AT ALL! And in a volatile investment time, sometimes zero can be the hero. In 2008, many investments lost a significant percentage of their principle; in some cases, the loss was nearly 40%. What if you had simply made zero in 2008? Zero is the hero!

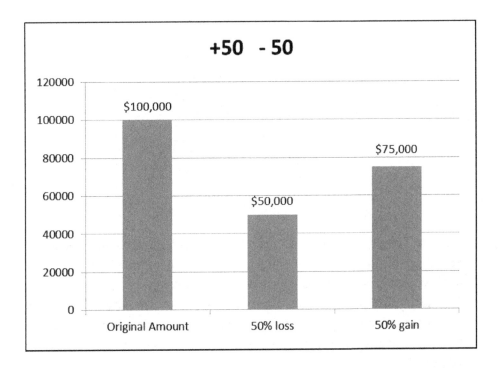

You may be wondering, "What is the likelihood of losing or earning 50% in any given year?" That's a really great question. Let's take a look at a little bit of recent history back to the years 2000, 2001, 2002, 2008, and take a look at the net losses to the S&P 500 Index. In 2008 alone, depending on when you measure, the markets tumbled approximately 40%. During the timeframe of 2000, 2001, and 2002, those same markets fell an additional 45%.

Historical S&P 500® Index Returns

Calendar Year	Return
2000	-10.14%
2001	-13.04%
2002	-23.37%
2003	26.38%
2004	8.99%
2005	3.00%
2006	13.62%
2007	3.53%
2008	-38.49%
2009	23.45%
2010	12.78%
2011	0.00%
2012	13.41%

It isn't much of a stretch to realize the devastating economic impact of these kinds of drops. Many of you have lived through them. There are many great people today still working who ought to be retired.

These losses seem to affect everybody equally. The results have been devastating to the average family. At a minimum, these economic markets and the turmoil have been discouraging to folks like us who are just trying to do the right thing!

So now, by using the above graph, you can see if in one year we make 50% and in the next year we lose 50%, it actually results in a 25% loss to our principal. I bet you didn't know it works this way! That is the purpose of **Money University**: to educate people about the compound effects of the market, taxes, and your own behavior!

Summary of Types of Individual Investment Vehicles

1. Traditional IRA accounts: this is such a broad topic, we could literally have an entire book just on this. An IRA account is any type of government-authorized retirement plan where the taxes are deferred on the front end and paid later in life. The IRA is not a type of investment vehicle. The IRA holds different types of investments. It is a defined-contribution plan that allows you to invest your money in various places. The actual IRA vehicle may hold stocks, bonds, mutual funds, commodities, real estate, and other cash equivalents. Here are a few limitations of the IRA that I have learned from my clients:
- Penalties and taxes prior to age 59½
- Taxation on required-minimum distributions past age 70½ may cause additional taxes on Social Security benefits
- Every distribution is fully taxable
- Taxable to your heirs
- Traditionally funded with mutual funds and stocks, which if left unattended could increase volatility during the roll-in

2. Traditional 401k accounts:
- Limited investment choices
- Can't contribute after leaving employment
- Fully taxable during retirement; same as IRA
- Full volatility to the market depending on individual choices

3. Stocks and bonds, market investments:
- Market Volatility
- Lack diversification if you buy just one stock
- Affected by things out of your control; potential to lose capital

4. Real Estate:
- Upkeep and expenses
- Reverse cash flow if not rented
- Disruption of rental income
- Limited liquidity

5. Commodities (Gold and Silver):
- Extreme market volatility
- May suffer the same or greater losses than stocks or bonds
- No readily-available secondary market
- Must convert to cash to use as currency
- Physical loss potential of the gold or silver itself
- Potential fraud

6. Banks and Credit Unions:
- Low interest rates
- Penalties for early withdrawal
- CDs are taxable in the year you *earn* the interest not in the year you *spend* the interest

7. Mutual Funds:
- Market volatility
- Upfront commissions may limit desire to make necessary trades or exchanges
- Many funds stay in the market even if it's going down

It may sound like almost everything is negative, but I want to assure you that it is not the case. It is important to understand both the pros and the cons of each of the investment and retirement strategies. The bigger of the problems with each of these areas generally falls in the lap of the purchaser: you!

I have witnessed many people who buy based on radio and TV-generated market hysteria. They wait until they hear about it in the media, and THEN buy after the price has gone up. We call that "buy high and sell low." There is a better way. Still, the ultimate success or failure will depend on your own behavior starting today.

The Most Common Reasons
People Don't Retire Well

1. Buying and selling investments emotionally

2. Procrastination and letting time slip through their fingers

3. Panic—looking for the hot stock that will erase years of financial sin

4. Having a short-term outlook on a long-term investment

5. Buying investments because they are popular, usually after they've gone way up in price

6. Not understanding the tax ramifications of investing

7. Becoming a do-it-yourselfer with products and services that normally require a license and take years to understand

8. Bailing out your adult children and family members time after time, never letting them suffer their own consequences ("Did he really say that? I am not sure if I like this guy!")

Investments are just like any other product. You should do your homework before investing, and make sure you understand all the risks and rewards. There is no such thing as the perfect investment. Get all the information, get a second opinion, and proceed with caution.

Your behavior counts in all of this. Staying the course rather than bailing out at the first sign of adversity seems to play a role. Not having a clear focus toward your goals has some impact. Having too much money can be a detriment also.

WHAT? Yes, having too much money, too quick, and not creating a consistent mindset about your money can be one of the most destructive things to happen to you. Consider what happens to those folks who acquire money too easily.

Wanna know why most of the NFL, NBA, and lottery winners are broke very quickly after acquiring their money? The next chapter discusses the wealth mindset, and how it affects the outcome. I was surprised when I learned these facts!

Chapter Five
Behavior Counts

(Why Most Lottery Winners and NFL Football Players Go Broke Within Five Years)

Rule: It doesn't matter how much you make, it matters how much you keep

The allure of sudden and new money is intoxicating. The idea of almost-unlimited money coming into your possession invokes many conversations around our country. Have you ever had a conversation that started like this?

- *"If I had $1 million..."*
- *"If I won the lottery I would...."*
- *"If money were no object..."*

Of course you have! We all have. In fact, I find it to be a very enjoyable exercise in values to have this conversation with your spouse or significant other. *"Sweetheart, if money were no object, what would you do with your life?"* I believe these kinds of conversations are healthy if done in the right context. I truly believe—with everything in me—that anybody can accomplish anything that they set their mind to. So, if it is your intent to have $1 million, perfect! If your conversations are merely wishful thinking, perhaps this type of talk will only lead you down the road to frustration and blame. I hope that's not the case for you.

I've been fortunate to work with some high-level athletes as they progress through their careers. I've also had the enriching education to work with many people who come into large sums of money rather quickly. I want to offer you a piece of advice right away, should you come into a large sum of money rather quickly. This advice will help you navigate the muddy waters ahead of you.

> **If you ever get one million dollars, the first thing you should do is become a millionaire!**

You may think I'm crazy by stating the obvious. But I believe the first thing you should do if you come into a large sum of money is learn to **think like millionaires do**. You need to learn to act like millionaires do. You need to actually become a person with a millionaire mind. Some people believe that they will get the money and then behave like a millionaire. I've got news for you:

> **In order to become a millionaire, you must act, think, and behave like a millionaire.**

How then, does a wealthy person act that is different from a non-wealthy person? Here is a brief list of behaviors that I witnessed consistently from normal people that others would deem to be successful. These lessons I witnessed were so very basic that anyone can copy them. Remember, the Lord our God loves the rich and the poor equally; there is no difference in them as people. Their wealth merely reflects a behavior around money. Money success doesn't make people good or bad. Having money or not having money doesn't determine your value as a person. It simply describes the values that you have accumulated over the course of your lifetime because of, and only because of, your actions relating to the resources that you have had at your disposal all of your life.

Wealthy people...
* Save money on a regular basis
* Use a team of professionals to guide them
* Make an effort to understand income taxes
* Don't take unnecessary risks
* Understand that wealth can come and go, and they seek to protect themselves and their families for long-term

Don't make the same mistakes that so many people have made before you. Here are a few I've noticed in my lifetime that led to the demise of people who have lost a lot of money.

It will amaze you how "the rich and famous" squander their money. ***Perspective Moment***: The people of lesser-developed countries cannot understand how YOU have squandered the money you have made. Remember, you earn millions in your own lifetimes. It isn't what you make; it is what you keep. Take a look:

Why NFL Players Really Go Bankrupt

FoxNews
By Ty Schalter,
NFL National Lead Writer
May 30, 2012

When Raghib "Rocket" Ismail signed the richest contract in football history, he thought he was set for life. But as he told Sports Illustrated, Ismail's then unheard-of $4.55 million salary disappeared almost as fast as he earned it. "I looked at my bank statement,"he said, "and I ju st went, 'What the...?'"

It seems impossible for multimillionaire athletes to go broke. However, Sports Illustrated found that after two years of retirement, 78 percent of NFL players are bankrupt or under financial stress. How can that be possible?

There are many contributing factors to the suddenly wealthy becoming suddenly living hand-to-mouth again. Horrific spending habits, bad investments, generosity and child support can put the wealthiest athlete into the poor house.

Spending

The most outrageous story of an athlete going broke doesn't come from the NFL. The NBA's Antoine Walker earned over $100 million during his career, but was arrested in 2009 for writing bad checks. What happened to his nine-figure fortune?

He spent it all....

Bad Investments

Baltimore Colts legend Johnny Unitas was one of the greatest quarterbacks ever to play the game. Unfortunately, his ahead-of-his-game field management skills didn't translate to the boardroom. He used his career earnings to buy ownership of "a chain of bowling establishments, a prime-rib restaurant, an air-freight company and Florida real estate investment." ...

Child Support

Former Denver Broncos tailback Travis Henry has famously fathered nine children by nine different women....

Generosity

Former Detroit Lions defensive tackle Luther Elliss has a problem providing for his many children, too: the five biological children he's fathered with his wife, and the six children they've adopted, some of whom have special needs....

Lessons Learned

Elliss told the Deseret News:

"It's not just professional athletes that are doing this. Look at our country-it's trillions in debt. Where are we going? We're still spending. It's something I've been advocating recently, especially at younger levels, we need to educate them in the basic finances and understanding you can't spend more than what you make."

While teams, the NFL and the NFLPA offer plenty of resources for players, many aren't thinking about how short most pro careers are. If most weren't convinced they were going to succeed, they likely wouldn't be in the pros to begin with.

Many Americans spend everything they earn, whether that's $25,000 a year or a $25 million signing bonus. But as dangerous as that is for regular Joes, it's even more so for the pros whose earning power is always one snap away from disappearing.

No matter how today's NFL players choose to spend their money, they need help saving enough to sustain themselves when those game checks stop coming.

Are these unusual cases? Nope. According to a 2009 Sports Illustrated article, 60 percent of former NBA players are broke within five years of retirement. 78% of former NFL players have gone bankrupt or are under financial stress after two years of retirement.

Is your current attitude about money moving you toward wealth?

"Formerly wealthy people"…

- Think the money will come in forever
- Don't pay attention to what they're spending
- Would rather look wealthy rather than *be* wealthy
- Have a "right now" vision instead of a long-term perspective
- Have no idea where their money has gone
- Have no accountability

Do you have any of the above symptoms in your life? Do you have any of these attitudes in your current life?

Are there any areas that you know deep down inside that you must improve?

Have you been a good steward of the resources currently in your life?

What would you be willing to change today that you might be financially independent ten or more years down the road?

I learned that wealth is generally a decision one makes on a moment-by-moment basis about how they are to spend the next amount of time or money. The wealthy don't care what they look like. They care about true security for themselves and their families. They want to make sure that there are enough resources to live for a lifetime. What about you? Do you have a day-to-day mentality about money? Or do you desire a long-term prosperity mindset, like most millionaires?

2020 Challenge!

I am completing this book in the year 2015. In five short years it will be the year 2020! That is approximately five years from right now. My question for you is do you have a 2020 vision?

This might be a great place for you to start when it comes to gathering wealth. This could be an epic moment for you and your family where the whole thing turns around. Where will you be five years from today? What steps will you take? What sacrifices are you willing to make? Would it be worth it this time? Where have you DECIDED to be when your birthday rolls around in 2020?

Remember:

- Small behaviors create BIG results...both Positive AND Negative
- If you save a dollar a day from age 18 until age 65 and earn 9% per year, you could accumulate an additional $228,804 dollars! Small behaviors create BIG results
- If you gain two pounds per year after high school (Guys only!) your formerly 150-pound athletic frame will be weighing in at 244 pounds at retirement! Small behaviors create BIG results...literally!
- The slight edge in behavior will make all the difference for you. Right now, this very moment, there is somebody on this planet who is rooting for you to get it right. There is somebody waiting for you to take the reins of this moment and accelerate forward. There is somebody who very much deserves success and so much more. That person is ...YOU!

Chapter Six Money Do's:
The Eleven Rules of Engagement

Rule: Love is grand. Divorce is a hundred grand. Get it right the first time!

"And do you Gary Groom, take Darla Debt to be your lawfully wedded wife for better or worse?"

"*Uh, I do?*"

Somewhere in there is the phrase "till death do us part." Perhaps they should restate that to read, till "debt" do us part!

> **I believe one of the most difficult parts of any marriage is money and finance. One of the major causes of stress in any marriage can often be traced back to money. I believe a sound, well-articulated financial plan is essential in any relationship. Relationships are tough enough without the extra pressure of a crummy financial life.**

Ask any pastor at any church in North America if there is any truth to the above statement. Ask them what some of their more common conversations are within their congregation. I believe that you will find many marriages suffering from a disease that is preventable and curable and fixable. Why volunteer for misery?

Why It Is Difficult

When we enter into marriage, it is generally one of the happiest moments of our life! From the time we are children, until that magical moment at the altar, we imagine what marriage might be like. We imagine the most beautiful wedding, a wonderful house, bubbly children, and a carefully examined life.

Unfortunately, those fantasies of the perfect life rarely reveal the price tag with them. Weddings today cost $50,000! A new house can be a quarter of a million dollars. The cost of educating a child has soared over $100,000. And if we put all of these things on credit cards, the price escalates even more by the interest rate. The very things that brought us joy in the planning bring us agony when we have to deal with the price tag.

Many things that bring us JOY in planning cause us ANGUISH in the implementation!

Wouldn't it make sense to establish some guidelines and rules for your marriage? Would you be better off knowing that you and your spouse are in agreement when it comes to things related to money?

I have some great friends here in Austin, Texas whose marriage exemplifies the right way to deal with money. The husband is a doctor, and the wife works at an executive job. They consult with each other on any occasion where more than $20 is being spent! I think that is a fantastic idea that all of us can learn from. Mutual planning and mutual respect mean no financial surprises! *What behaviors can you implement that might actually prevent bickering and worrying over money?*

Let's take a look at a few ideas that can pave a smooth path for your marriage financially:

1. Decide who controls the checkbook; only one person should be writing checks in the marriage

2. Only one person pays the bills; usually the person who controls the checkbook should pay the bills

3. Prepare and live by a budget the first year of marriage

4. For the remaining 99 years of marriage, prepare and live by a budget

5. Set spending limits for which no approval is required

6. Decide in advance if both partners will work

7. If one of the partners is the self-employed, entrepreneurial type, will the other partner work in a steady job to provide some level of security?

8. Pay yourself first; if this is not doable, rewrite your entire budget until it is doable; this is the single most important thing any individual or couple could ever do; make this an enduring habit that will benefit you for your lifetime; it is a behavior that your children will surely model

9. Charity. Tithing. Giving. What role will your spiritual and societal beliefs play in your financial life? For many, the tithe is given first prior to even paying yourself first; having an ethic of charitable interest will always keep your financial life in the right perspective; being able to help others will most assuredly make you feel the right kind of wealthy

10. Establish guidelines for money and children, i.e., private school, college, etc.

11. Write a thorough financial plan that includes life insurance, getting your wills completed, and complete any name changes; make sure beneficiaries from previous programs benefit your new spouse; most of all, seek wise counsel—ask your advisor to help you stay accountable to your plans. Stick with it!

Marriage Resources and Fun Things to Do

Blessings and events jar. This is one of the neatest things I've ever seen from one of the editors of this book. She and her husband keep a jar on their mantel. They keep a small notepad and a pen by the jar and every time a significant or fun event happens in their life they write it down fold the piece of paper and toss it into the jar. At the end of each year they sit down with each other and read over all the blessings that they've enjoyed during the previous year. I believe the ability to count your blessings and focus on the positives is one of the single best things you can do, not just in marriage, but in life. Thank you, Autumn and Rob, for the privilege of witnessing excellent behavior on a regular basis!

Trip fund. If you are meeting your responsibilities and have disposable income, why not set a few dollars aside every month to take a wonderful trip or anniversary celebration? A few dollars here and a few dollars there add up very quickly and I believe it is vital in a new marriage (or any other marriage for that matter) to have something to look forward to. Have a fun trip at the end of the time. When you've worked hard, this can be a fantastic celebration to help the two of you commit to reaching meaningful goals. Plus, you can add your trip memories to the Blessings Jar!

Baby retirement fund. This changes the world. ***Knowing*** it does **NOTHING** to change the world. ***Doing this changes the world***. What kind of advantage would it give your child if you are able to put $1,000 away for them on the day they were born? Not college money. Not wedding money. Retirement money! Is this something you should be thinking about?

The answer is an overwhelming yes! $1,000 put away at 9% for seventy years could yield your newborn baby an extra $400,000 in retirement! Isn't that the kind of legacy you would like to leave for your newborn baby?

$1,000 put away in a "baby retirement fund" that is left until age seventy and earns 9% annually would grow to $416,730!

Have a weekly board meeting with you and your spouse. Discuss worries, goals, accomplishments, and above all, love on each other during this process. The world can be a tough place. This meeting can be a wonderful time to reconnect, recover, dream, or just enjoy each other's company. It is essential to communicate between spouses on a regular basis. **Treasure these times**. It is a wealth that cannot be taken away and is an immeasurable gift.

Save your change for something special. Let this be a habit from your first day of marriage. You could save it for a trip. You could save it for your tenth anniversary. You can save it for almost any occasion, but let's take a quick moment and look at the math (we will discuss this later in a section called "Save a Large Gob of Cash").

Let's say that you got married at the age of twenty-five and you and your spouse were able to save $25 per month just in coins. Assuming you could earn a 9% interest rate and chose to invest those coins monthly, how much money might you accumulate toward your goals just by saving coins? Here is a quick graph on why it is so important to "***Keep the Change!***"

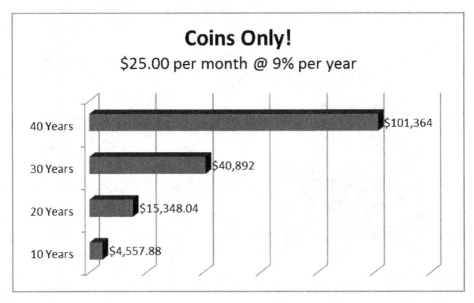

Coins Only!
$25.00 per month @ 9% per year

- 40 Years — $101,364
- 30 Years — $40,892
- 20 Years — $15,348.04
- 10 Years — $4,557.88

Disclaimer: All hypothetical, of course. No investment returns implied guaranteed, estimated, suggested, etc. This is just a mathematical example. If you don't like it, give your change to a cause that you appreciate.

Did I ever mention my grandmother to you? She used to have this saying that we lived by in our family: *"Every little extra $101,364 you have at age sixty-five will come in handy!"*

Do you think this is something you can teach your children? What if on the day you were born, your parents began saving $25 per month for you? And what if at your age of eighteen, you carried that $25 a month habit all the way through the age of seventy? What might that simple little investment **behavior** yield for you at your retirement age of seventy?

$25 per month/9% annual return/seventy years = $1,385,766.

This is a *__behavior-driven solution,__* not an investment-driven solution. It simply takes time and consistency. Anyone can do this. Mathematics works for EVERYBODY!

This is the change the author saved while at the hotel during the completion of this book. Even while holed up for less than one week, he accumulated about $10.00!

So, let's summarize what we know so far. Being married is tough. Understanding money is tough. Putting those two things together is sort of like what happens when an unstoppable force hits an immoveable object. It can get pretty complicated! If you have ever just wanted to pull your hair out, welcome to the same stuff that your parents went through.

We can now take a look forward since we have taken the appropriate look backward. We haven't done a great job as a country. But that is about to change. And YOU will be a great part of that change.

The next chapter details deep insight as to how the successful families have made it in this country. Besides hard work, how did they make it? "What did they know that I didn't know?" Have you ever said, "The rich get richer and the poor get poorer?" Well, that is absolutely true! And the healthy stay healthier, and so on. Those euphemisms are true because they are all built upon behavior.

Chapter Seven talks about behavior. It doesn't take education or money to decide on a behavior. Get ready to win, not from luck, but from decision.

Chapter Seven
Success Leaves Clues: Five Steps (Clues) to a Winning Plan

Rule: It is Actually Okay to Copy Off the Person Sitting Next to You

In this chapter, you change the world. Really.

It has often been stated, **"You must become the change that you wish to see in this world."** How many times in your life have you ever wished that your situation would've turned out differently? Have you ever wondered what it would have been like to be born wealthy? What would it feel like for you to have a confident financial life as you grow older?

The answer is really pretty simple. Have you ever thought about asking somebody how they went about accomplishing the very things that you yourself would like to accomplish? Wouldn't it be great if somebody who was living the life that you'd like to live were willing to share their secrets of success? Consider it done!

For the past thirty years, I have worked with a variety of individuals and families as they prepare, manage, and create their finances for the future. These clients have come in all shapes and sizes, from all backgrounds, and from varying degrees of success. Over the three decades that I have helped people plan and prepare their financial lives, I have noticed a few common threads among these families. The steps we are about to discuss are common among financially successful people. To the successful, these five steps are very basic, in fact, almost habits. And it is our habits that make all the difference. In our lives, first we form our habits. Then our habits create outcomes. Are there financial habits you would like to change? Are there financial things you would like to teach your children as well?

Coming from a small town, it was inevitable that at some point one of my relatives would also be one of my schoolteachers. In the third grade, my mother's distant cousin, Dorothy, was ill-advisedly assigned to be my homeroom teacher. Since I knew her as a family member, I suspected that I might be able to get by with a few more shenanigans than just the average student. During our math assignment, I continually copied off the smartest kid in the class, Joe Mark Cowden. This guy was good, and I was a fairly lazy third-grader. It just made sense to me that I would copy his answers since he had already gone to all the trouble to figure it out! It made no sense to me to reinvent the wheel.

> **Successful people are willing to do those things that less-successful people are simply unwilling to do!**

Aunt Dorothy had a very <u>different</u> perspective when she caught me *"borrowing"* other people's work. Because we were in a small town, she had an unrelenting fear of showing favoritism toward me, and more than doubled my punishment when she caught me cheating. Here is what I learned from that lesson: <u>copying from somebody else who is successful is a high form of praise</u>. Cheating, on the other hand, will get you five horrible swats from the principal, chalkboard cleaning duty, and a stern talking to from a distant relative who seriously questioned whether I would turn out to be an okay citizen.

RULE: cheating is bad; emulating positive and uplifting behavior is great! Knowing the difference is called wisdom.

> **Thank you, Aunt Dorothy, for setting me straight on this matter in your gentle and loving way. I appreciate the interest you took in my well being, and helping shape me into the man I would be proud for you to know!**

If you have successful people in your life who will share their tips with you, that is fantastic. Very often in our culture, people don't like to talk about money, religion, or politics. (Actually, the internet has changed our desire to talk about politics—it seems now <u>everybody</u> has a well-documented, public political opinion!) The following five steps are not things that I read in a book. These are not items that you will find somewhere on the internet. In fact, the formation and recognition of these five items, and the order in which they occur, took me nearly three decades of observation to understand.

You can learn these steps in a matter of hours. They work, and they work better if you use them in the right order.

You wouldn't put the roof on a house until the walls were built, right? You wouldn't put icing on the cake prior to baking it, right? (Silly example I know ... everyone eats the icing first!) What time and wisdom will teach you, if you are paying close attention, is that there is a distinct order in setting up your financial house too.

Before you would ever build a house you would go through many preliminary steps to make sure the house was just like you wanted it. You would pick a neighborhood, a piece of land, hire your builder, review a floor plan, and many other related issues. Later, as the house is built, you would pick out paint color, décor, and garage door openers. This is the logical order in building a house. So, what is the logical order for YOUR financial house? Did YOU eat the icing before the cake was baked (new car, debt, etc.)?

We call these the Five Steps—the Five Clues, the Five Things, High Five, the Five-O'clock News. I know it is pretty simple and that there are other people who believe in highly-complex mathematical equations to building your financial house. But these are the steps I have seen a multitude of successful people use to win the financial game. Yes, it is okay to copy from their previously-successful work.

Aunt Dorothy would approve.

Enrich your life forever by implementing thirty years of lessons in just a few short hours.

Clue # 1: Vision—A Clear Vision of What You Want

If you are casual about your goals, and casual about your dreams, you might find that you have become a *casual*ty! The more specific you are about your objectives, the more likely it is that you will accomplish them. You wouldn't take a trip without having a destination in mind, right? This financial trip you are on is exactly the same way. You must assess your starting point accurately and you must determine an ending point. That ending point could be your retirement date or the date by which you would like to have children, or the date by which you would like to build your dream home.

The vision portion of your financial plan is not just about wants and desires. It also must include the speed bumps along the way—like inflation, taxes, or any other item that might interrupt your plan.

Of course this portion of your plan is extremely flexible and may change on a daily basis. Life has a way of helping us focus on what is truly important.

What other item should be included in your vision plan? Children? Charity? A waterslide in the backyard? A bat pole in your house? What is it exactly that you are trying to accomplish from a financial standpoint during your working years? What about leaving a legacy or creating an educational foundation? Perhaps you would like for your work to benefit your church at some point in your life. How might you best accomplish that? These are the types of questions that you should be asking yourself as you begin your financial plan.

Retirement Planning: We make millions of dollars in our lifetime. We just don't keep very many of them!

Have you ever just thought, "Where does all the money go?"

The statistics in America are just terrible. With eighty million baby boomers hurtling toward retirement without a plan, the need for good retirement planning has never been greater. For the over-sixty-five population, the compound effects of inflation and a volatile market have left the wrong kind of dent in the universe. Too many people live below our nation's poverty line after retirement. Too many people struggle financially at a time when they can least afford it. These years, often referred to as the Golden Years, don't seem to have much gold in them. In fact, I think we could look at the current situation for much of America as the "Tarnished Years." Those who avoided calamity usually had a plan in place. In an earlier chapter, we discussed the plight of my dad, Charles, as he went from $200-a-month sack boy at the grocery store, to $500 per month at the Rock Island railroad, to $1,000 a month as a retiree. If you would, just put on your 1965 glasses for a moment and walk through this journey with me.

Getting a pay raise from $200 a month to $500 a month seemed astronomically large at the time. And while his pay continued to rise as he continued with the railroad, his Rock Island pension remained level to some degree. In fact, he is lucky to have his pension given that the Rock Island suffered terrible financial difficulty. If you told Charles in 1965 that he would be able to retire on $1,000 a month in the future that probably looked pretty good to a young father of three children. The problem here is that neither my father nor the Rock Island had a clear vision plan for the future. Very simply, they didn't allocate for inflation. These are the type of speed bumps that must be included in your vision plan.

How much money will you need during retirement? If your vision plan can include at least a minimal retirement, I think we are off to a great start. Because so many people fail at this one provision, I think it is absolutely vital that we lock down your retirement plan first, and have this as a high priority as a family. Let's make sure that your retirement will be secure and somewhat predictable before we go buying any yachts, helicopters, or waterslides. Deal?

As we continue on the path of creating your Vision Plan, let's do a quick scenario where we factor in inflation and try to determine what we will call *"your number."* When we enter kindergarten and first grade, our teachers desperately strive to teach us our phone number! I remember as a young child, my kindergarten teacher Miss Martha Jones asking me, "Cash, do you know your number?" It is amazing to me that we are still asking the same questions of people who are forty and fifty years old! So let me ask, do you know your number? In 1966, my phone number was *273-3170.* Oddly enough, my financial number today is *$2,733,170*. (Actually, I am just trying to make you smile a bit as we head into these pivotal chapters…it is more fun to learn if you are smiling!)

Here is a simple mathematical equation to understand your number. We must make one assumption—that you are living on the right amount of money today, and are at least surviving.

Step 1:	Answer this question: at what age would you genuinely like to retire, and make work optional?	
Step 2:	How many years is that from now?	
Step 3:	(*assuming age sixty-five is your answer*) If you were age sixty-five today, how much money would you need to have walking in the door each month to live the type of life that you have imagined? (*in today's dollars*)	$
Step 4:	Estimate how much Social Security will provide toward this number	$
Step 5:	At what rate do you believe inflation will occur between today and your age 65?	%

Assumptions: $5,000 per month current income, 3% inflation, and current age is forty, which is twenty-five years until age sixty-five.

At your age sixty-five, it will take $10,468 per month to pay for what $5,000 pays for today. So, to retire at age sixty-five and live like you do today will take $10,468 per month walking in the door each month from age sixty-five forward. Assuming that Social Security will provide $3,000 of that amount (check your own statements for a more exact estimate), then your NET MINIMUM RETIREMENT INCOME MUST BE $7,468 PER MONTH.

THE CONCEPT OF DRAWDOWN. Take a moment here. The concept of drawdown is _**vital**_ to your success. It is a very simple concept, but a very necessary concept.

**Drawdown is this**: the amount of money you can prudently take **from** your investment accounts to live on the rest of your life. The basic idea is to create a pool of money from which you can draw regular income. The account that your drawdown amount comes from should be minimally risky, and hopefully not subject to wild market fluctuations.

Let's assume your retirement account has $200,000 in it. Depending on whom you ask the safe drawdown amounts are anywhere between 3 and 5%. For this discussion, I will use 5% as a potential- drawdown amount (I am not saying that it is possible, I am just using it as a hypothetical example).

$200,000 x .05 (5%) = $10,000 per year as a "Drawdown Amount"

Pretty simple, right? There is some assumption that the $200,000 might grow depending on where you have it saved or invested. We are now in the _**income phase**_ and no longer in the _**accumulation phase.**_ A potential set of negative years in the market might be devastating to your account where your drawdown is taking place. We will address this more in section four on _investing_, but for now, we are using this just as a formula to understand the principle of drawdown.

You need $7,468 per month to hit your retirement goal. That actually adds up to $89,616 per year. You must take this $89,616 **from** your retirement account. The next step is to divide $89,616 by .05 (5% drawdown amount). In just a moment, we will know the exact amount of money you will need to accomplish your retirement goal:

$89,616 ÷ .05 = $1,792,320

$1,792,320 is your number!

> **If you had $1,792,320 in an account earning/withdrawing 5% per year, you could withdraw $89,616 per year, which is exactly $7,468 per month, which at your future age sixty-five is exactly the same as the $5,000 per month you earn right now. Whew!**

Of course there are many other factors when configuring your number. Make sure you work closely with your advisor or CPA as you work toward establishing a firm goal. Do not be discouraged by this number. Time is actually on your side, but it is important to get started now.

As we finish with the section on vision planning, keep the book of Proverbs in mind where it states:

> **"Where there is no vision the people perish."**

There are many other things to consider in your vision plan, but retirement seems to be the one that most people neglect. Given that time and money are equally important, it is time, right now, to get started!

Clue # 2: Prevent Irreversible Mistakes

In this chapter, we will learn how to protect yourselves and your family.

We spoke of the Four Dreaded Horsemen of your financial life a few pages ago. In this chapter, we expand on some of the risks and how to mitigate them. Many of these risks are self-imposed behaviors usually stemming from apathy or the false belief that there is no perceived importance of the item at hand. Let's dig a little deeper and see if any of these monsters are under your financial bed.

First, let's define irreversible mistakes. An irreversible mistake is a mistake you cannot reverse—plain and simple. Here are some mistakes that come to mind, all of which are preventable. Once you have made the decision to avoid these problems, worry diminishes, and you can move forward with much confidence.

Irreversible Mistake:
Lack of a Properly-Executed Will Package

This is not legal advice. This is life advice. The will package is much more than just your ordinary will. It is all the items and documents that help make that part of your life bulletproof. For example, it is important to not only have your will set up, but want to have a rock-solid plan in place.

Visit with your attorney or estate planning attorney and make sure each of these items is in place:

- Medical power of attorney
- Durable power of attorney
- Directive to physicians
- Advance medical directives
- Passwords and lock-box keys
- Custodial issues for minor children
- Special needs trust for special needs children

These are but a few of the things that you'll want to take care of with your legal team. Make sure you get all of your legal questions answered by a licensed, competent attorney with whom you have good rapport. It is also important to make sure each of these documents is updated as the situation warrants.

If you are the kind of person who is a little intimidated by attorneys (like me), there is a wonderful resource in our country that may very well be the best thing since sliced bread!

A few years back I ran across a service called LegalShield that seemed to meet most of the needs of my family AND my clientele. They have been around since 1972 and have a wonderful reputation in the market.

LegalShield operates sort of like an HMO for doctors. For somewhere around $20 a month they will give you access to well qualified attorneys in your area for most legal questions, business or personal, just by having a membership. I like that it is month-to-month (no long term contracts) and covers a wide array of legal situations across the United States. I have used it personally to review contracts, fight traffic tickets (for my wife), and to politely ask my neighbors barking dogs to tone it down after midnight.

Here's the part that really amazed me: as a member they prepared a will for me and my wife, medical powers of attorney, advanced medical directives and all the other worrisome stuff at no extra charge. That's RIGHT! FREE WILL!

If you don't already have an existing relationship with an attorney that you love, then I would strongly encourage you to find a local representative of this company to help facilitate your needs. You can find a representative in your area by visiting "http://www.LegalShield.com."

Irreversible Mistake:
Not Buying the Right Amount of Life Insurance

Using the drawdown concept discussed earlier, it is a prudent and protective move to own life insurance that would protect your family in the event of your premature death. There are many questions about life insurance we should answer. How much life insurance is enough? What is the right kind of life insurance? How long do I need this insurance to cover me and my family?

Consider this: A report by LIMRA indicated that the average overall death payout from a life insurance policy in America was under $90,000. If your family received a check for $90,000, and you took a drawdown of 5% a year, how much would a $90,000 life insurance policy pay your family in the coming years? Answer: $4,500 per year (assuming a 5% drawdown). Is that what you wanted when you bought the insurance policy?

It is important to buy the right amount; generally twenty times your annual salary to make sure your family has enough money in the event of your premature death. Is your family protected?

Irreversible Mistake:
Paying Off Your Mortgage Early

Homeownership is one of the greatest American dreams. For most people, a mortgage is a necessary tool required to own a home. Most families simply don't have enough money saved to pay cash for a house and that may not be a good idea anyway. Most mortgage loans today cost between 3.5% and 4.5%.

Let's take a look at why people suggest paying off a mortgage early. Let's assume that you have a $225,000 mortgage on your house at an interest rate of 4% and you're making payments over a 30-year (360 months) period of time. Your estimated mortgage payment would be $1074 per month.

Should you take your mortgage full-term and pay all 360 payments, at the end of your mortgage, you would have paid $386,706 for your $225,000 home! That is a total of $161,706 of mortgage interest paid over the life of the loan. There are many people who would look at this and proclaim it to be a bad thing. Rather than reacting on emotion, let's apply simple mathematics using some basic assumptions.

First, what if we took the traditional advice and added $150 per month to our mortgage payment with the idea that we could pay our loan off early? These additional payments would indeed pay our mortgage off early. By paying an additional $150 per month, we would pay our mortgage off in 285 months, or 23.75 years. This would save us seventy-five payments of $1,074, for a total savings of $80,550!

This may look like a substantial savings and almost seems inarguable that this would be the way to go. Once again, let's apply mathematics, not emotion, and answer this question: what ELSE could we do with that $150 a month that might bring us similar or possibly greater value? What if you were able to invest that SAME $150 per month ($1,800 annually for 23.75 years @ 9% per year)? At the end of the exact same period, you WOULD HAVE accumulated

$134,849 of ACTUAL CASH in some type of savings or investment account that you control directly! At the end of 23.75 years, you would owe approximately $75,000 on your mortgage. You could take the cash you accumulated, pay the mortgage off, and have an additional $60,000 left over. Yikes! The public perception, based on this mathematical example, is put mildly, WRONG!

While one way looks preferable, the fact is, the mathematics do not support paying your mortgage off early in this method that we call *"inside the mortgage."* Believing the contrary way, we call paying it off *"outside the mortgage."* Mortgage money right now is very cheap. It is also very tax-deductible for most people. To pay off low-interest tax-deductible money with other monies that might earn a higher interest rate makes no sense.

Consider these other issues with paying off your mortgage early:

- Equity is not cash; equity cannot be used to pay utilities to invest with or even buy a cup of coffee
- Equity does not earn a rate of return

- Equity is absolutely not liquid; in an emergency, would you rather have equity or cash? If you lost your job would you rather have equity or cash? If you had a family emergency or medical emergency would you rather have equity or cash?
- How do you get cash out of an equity real estate position? You must either sell the house, or get a new loan. If you are in a position where your health or job has been compromised, either of these two previous methods may not be available to you

Don't be house rich and cash poor!

Here is one caveat that is very important. If you are not disciplined with money, if you spend everything that comes in and save nothing, if you consider yourself irresponsible, then paying off your mortgage may very well make the most sense. Managing your mortgage is much like managing any other financial instrument. It takes practical application, discipline, and a steady hand at the wheel. The key is to keep moving forward. Paying your mortgage off early is a good idea if you aren't committed to the idea of saving extra money in some other type of investment. Both are good; one is just better than the other.

Irreversible Mistake:
I Can't Even Say It—It Is Too Egregious

Each year, my wife and I go through our budget and take a look back at how we earned money and how we spent money. A few years back, I found a budget item that became a "*deep curiosity*" for me. I found out that my wife had been overpaying the electric bill every month for the last fifteen years! I couldn't believe it! Every single month for the previous fifteen years of our marriage, she had been sending our electric utility company and additional $250 per month! Wow! We had what I will call an "interesting conversation" that went something like this:

Husband: "*Uh, why are you overpaying the electric bill $250 per month?*"

Wife: *"Because I'm afraid they will cut off electricity and I don't want to be left in the dark!"*

Husband: *"I'm sorry I still don't understand. Explain it to me some more."*

Wife: *"It really isn't that big of a deal. Every April they send me a full refund of the overpayments, so it's sort of like a savings account for us."*

Husband: *"Savings account? Does it pay an interest rate? Do we have access to it during the year?"*

Wife: *"Not really. But at least we know we get to keep the electricity turned on. And by the way, if you want to take over paying the bills, you may jump in at any time you see fit."*

Husband: ***"I'm beginning to see it your way, sweetheart!"***

This conversation never really happened about the electric bill. But I think you'd be shocked to find out that this conversation actually does happen in 86% of all of the taxpaying homes in the USA. In fact, we are not talking about the electric bill at all. We are talking about your income taxes. I believe one of the craziest things a family can do is to regularly overpay their income taxes. **Why would you *ever* overpay a bill that simply is not due?** It doesn't make you more patriotic. It doesn't make you less-likely to be audited. It just makes you more broke!

> ### Why would you *ever* overpay a bill that simply is not due?

There are times in life where the tax system lends itself to getting an occasional tax refund. But if you're getting a tax refund over $500 per year, and you're doing so on a regular basis—simply put, you are planning your taxes incorrectly. This is an irreversible mistake if done over the course of a lifetime. The average tax refund in North America is around $3,000 per year and 86% of the taxpaying families get these types of refunds. Is it any wonder that our population struggles financially? This type of behavior must be stopped immediately and at all cost. If you are a voluntary bill over-payer... Stop it!

- You lose the purchasing value of your money
- Your cash flow goes down
- You could be paying off other things or saving for the future
- Your money earns zero interest, not to mention the effects of inflation
- Waiting around for your money to show back up is the worst form of money management

If you do not know how to properly deal with your income taxes, seek the help of a professional tax advisor. These are the types of behaviors that linger in families for years and the compound effect can be devastating to the outcome of your financial life.

Remember, ***IT IS NOT HOW MUCH WE MAKE; IT IS HOW MUCH WE KEEP***! And if you keep sending extra money to the IRS for no apparent reason, you alone have made your financial road more difficult.

Other Irreversible Mistakes:

- Lack of disability income planning
- Long-term care issues
- Macho men who run the family and leave a bereaved spouse alone to learn all of this during a time of grief (women are way too sweet and practical to ever do such a thing)

Clue # 3: Save a Large Gob of Cash

Rule number three, save a large gob of cash, is really not that exciting. It is pretty self-explanatory, really. And from the outside, this may seem like plain-vanilla advice. In a world of complex ideas, having an emergency fund ready for the unexpected, though very simple, is one of the single most important components of a well-orchestrated financial plan.

Take a moment right now and think back on the types of emergencies you have encountered in your life. Flat tire, broken refrigerator, loss of a job, illness, and the list goes on and on and on. Might there be other emergencies in your future? I believe the primary reason that good families end up in BAD DEBT is that *Step 3, Save a Large Gob of Cash*, has been skipped or forgotten to some degree. Don't ignore this step. It is VITAL to your well being and peace of mind to have the right kind of reserves. Taking care of this step will make you feel better and be better prepared for the road to come.

How much is enough? Like most answers, it depends. For some, two-three months of reserve is enough. Others are more comfortable with more. There are multiple ways to begin to accumulate cash. Here we illustrate a few budgeting and cash-accumulation ideas that might help you get started:

Budgeting Ideas

Simple things you can do today to save money!

1. Stop getting a tax refund and put those dollars into your monthly budget
2. Save a dollar a day starting today!
3. Save your change every day; each year, put these dollars into a long-term savings account
4. Borrow from your 401(k) to pay off higher-interest rate debts, credit cards, or obligations
5. Limit your 401(k) contribution to exactly the amount that is matched by your employer
6. Seek wisdom of prudent people; check out websites such as http://www.isavea2z.com
7. Drink water while out to dinner; then go home and deposit the exact amount you might have spent on drinks into some type of savings account
8. Lower your cell-phone bill to a program that is $50 per month or less
9. Go through your bank statements and find auto-draft items that you no longer use or enjoy; cancel those unused health club memberships, pet insurance programs, travel clubs, etc.
10. Refinance your house to a lower interest rate and an extended term if possible; consider using these funds to pay off debts; use a competent, licensed mortgage advisor to discuss options
11. Seek advice from a competent, licensed insurance professional about adjusting deductibles and other items on your various insurance plans

Clue # 4: Invest for the Future

Finally, we get to the fun stuff! Here we offer those bits of information that make guys like me the life of any cocktail party. (I've never actually been invited to a cocktail party, but should that trend reverse, I will proudly share this information). Before we get going, and to avoid confusion, I want to point out that the NEXT chapter (Chapter Eight) will go into more detail about specific investing philosophies. The design and purpose of this chapter is to explain the fourth rule of a winning plan, which is investing for the future.

Why We Invest in the First Place

As we all know by now, the negative impact of inflation is eroding our purchasing power. What cost one dollar today, will cost two dollars shortly down the road. It is a harsh reality that we may spend as much time during the retirement years (the income phase) as we did in the earning years (accumulation phase). Because of increased longevity of people, the retirement equation and the investment equation must be addressed adequately. We invest during the *accumulation phase*. We spend those investments during the *income phase.*

The rules of how our investments work, therefore, may be radically different during the income phase than they are in the accumulation phase. During the *accumulation phase*, downward market swings might actually be to our benefit as we continually contribute money into our accounts. But, during the *income phase*, we are no longer contributing new dollars toward our retirement. Generally, during this time, we are only taking money **out** of our retirement plan. Be advised and take action as the rules during the different phases are **very** different and require different actions on your part.

> **To succeed during the income and retirement phase, it will require you to change your perception of how and why to invest. The old rules and models no longer apply.**

Dollar Cost Averaging

This section will examine the concept of dollar cost averaging. This describes the potential impact of continually investing dollars over a long stretch of time so as to even out the highs and lows of a volatile market.

Let's take a look at the DCA concept, except let's use cows instead of dollars!

Let's go into the cow business. Start by investing $100.00 per month in cows for the next ten months. How will you feel in month five when the original price of cows has fallen nearly 50%?

Buying Cows Can Be A Moo-ving Experience!

Month	Investment	Price of Cows	# Purchased
1	$100	$10	10
2	$100	$9	11.11
3	$100	$8	12.5
4	$100	$7	14.29
5	$100	$6	16.66
6	$100	$5	20
7	$100	$6	16.67
8	$100	$7	14.29
9	$100	$8	12.50
10	$100	$10	10
TOTAL	$1000	—	138.01

What a ride! At month ten, you say to yourself, "I am getting out of the cow business, it is risky!" But wait; let's see what our return on investment is.

Cows started at $10, fell significantly, and then climbed back to $10. After ten months, we have spent $1,000 and have 138 cows. What is our rate of return on the overall investment if we sell right now?

First, determine the current market value of the overall investment:

138 cows @ $10 each = $1,380.

Now calculate your rate of return:

[(Portfolio Value – Investment) ÷ Investment] x 100

[($1,380 – 1,000) ÷ 1,000] x 100 = 38%

A 38% return rate is pretty great!

How does this work? Dollar cost averaging (DCA) is a strategy for evening out market highs and lows. By investing on a regular and consistent basis, you may purchase your investments at varying prices as well. For example, when the price of cows fell to $5 per cow, your contributions were buying twice as many cows!

Sometimes, investing consistently is more important than "how the market is doing."

Congratulations, you now understand Dollar Cost Averaging!

Disclaimer: This is only a mathematical example. **Money University** *does not sell cows. This implies no potential return of investment, rate of return, or actual experience. We made this up solely to teach dollar cost averaging. No cows were hurt in the writing of this example.*

While you're unlikely to see an example like the one above, it does serve as an excellent example of how volatility can be mitigated by regular investing ($10 cows vs. $5 cows).

The Basics of Investing

After working with clients from all walks of life, I have summarized the basics of investing successfully in the four basic areas:

1. **Get Started!** There is nothing more important than the act of starting
2. **Put your money in a good spot**. You don't need a bunch of crazy ideas designed to double your money overnight; you don't need to add a bunch of risk. Be reasonable!
3. **Watch over it**. Have meaningful conversations with your advisor. Ask lots of questions. Be involved in the process to a reasonable degree.

At a minimum, have an annual checkup with your money just like you would your health

4. **Understand taxes on your investments**. Not only can the market play a negative role in your investments, so will taxes. Make sure you understand your obligations tax-wise as you build your investment portfolio. The market will have periods of appreciation AND depreciation. However, the money given back to the tax system never returns to your portfolio

Investing Overview

In this process, you are learning the five clues to a solid financial plan. Investing is clue number four, and there is a reason it is in this order. The dollars saved in your emergency fund are just as important as the dollars saved in your investment portfolio. Why? Because when you have an emergency, you don't want to have to pull those kinds of dollars for a short-term emergency from a long-term investment account. That makes sense, right? Investments are long-term and emergencies are usually short-term. Doing these things out of order could wreck your financial plan. In just a moment, we will discuss the fifth step, Getting Out of Debt (G.O.O.D.)

Later in Chapter Eight, we will discuss various types of investing strategies that almost anyone can implement. There is a time and a place for each step. Understanding the order is just as important as anything you will learn.

Clue # 5: Get Out of Debt (G.O.O.D)

Rule: The borrower is a slave to the lender

Let's summarize the first four steps that we have learned in this chapter:

1. **We need a clear vision of what we want**. When we go to a restaurant, we order from a menu. You would never go and just say "bring me food." Having a vision is simply deciding what you would like for dinner, finding the recipe, putting the ingredients together, and then

enjoying the delicious meal you have made

2. **We must prevent terrible mistakes <u>before</u> they happen**. This is the yucky stuff that we must get past to avoid having to talk about it again! Nobody likes talking about death or disability or taxes. So wouldn't it be better for all of us if we dealt with it once at the front end, knowing that we have acknowledged and dealt with these potential risks, and done the very best job we can do, should something unforeseen happen?

3. **We must save a large gob of cash**. Step three, done correctly, will assist us in both steps four and five. You don't want to raid your investment account every time a car tire goes flat. The biggest reason we go in debt is because somewhere along the line, we skipped step three. Don't skip step three. It is vital!

4. **We must create a reasonable investment plan**. This is something long-term in nature, built on a reasonable understanding of our risk tolerance, and not a put-and-take account. It is in alignment also with our tax objectives

Let's introduce the fifth and final concept of the Five Clues to developing a strong financial plan. This concept is G.O.O.D.!

Get Out of Debt

First, let's establish a definition of good debt versus bad debt.

Good debt = tax-deductible, low-interest mortgage debt.

Bad debt = everything else. There are occasions where a low interest, defined term, car loan will be to your advantage. Having lots of payments, as a general rule, is a bad idea though.

If you have managed to accumulate cash, and you have begun a meaningful investment program, you might be wondering why you should invest **prior** to getting out of debt. That's a great question and I like to answer it very directly. There are other financial authors who believe you should get out of debt at all cost and as early as possible. I don't totally disagree with that. But I believe that missing a year of investing **today** has such an enormous negative impact **later** in life that it just makes sense to establish a good habit **now** (saving) to replace a bad habit (debt). The cost of waiting to invest is simply too high to put it off for another year.

By now, we've done a multitude of things that have improved our cash-flow position. Here is a brief summary of things you could do to increase your cash flow every month:

Simple things you can do today to save money!

Do these look familiar to you? They should! We talked about them a few chapters ago. See how all of these things are interwoven into your financial success? You can use your behaviors to pay off debt, to save money, to be better financially. These steps will help you "Save a Large Gob of Cash." These exact behaviors, once you have saved some money, will help you get and stay out of debt. It is a process.

1. Stop getting a tax refund and put those dollars into your monthly budget
2. Save a dollar a day starting today!
3. Save your change every day. Each year, put these dollars into a long-term savings account
4. Borrow from your 401(k) to pay off higher interest rate debts, credit cards, or obligations
5. Limit your 401(k) contribution to exactly the amount that is matched by your employer
6. Seek wisdom of prudent people. Check out websites such as http://www.isavea2z.com
7. Drink water while out to dinner. Then go home and deposit the exact amount you might have spent on drinks into some type of savings account
8. Lower your cell-phone bill to a program that is $50 per month or less
9. Go through your bank statements and find auto-draft items that you no longer use or enjoy; cancel those unused health club memberships, pet

insurance programs, travel clubs, etc.

10. Refinance your house to a lower interest rate and an extended term if possible; consider using these funds to pay off debts; use a competent, licensed mortgage advisor to discuss options

11. Seek advice from a competent, licensed insurance professional about adjusting deductibles and other items on your various insurance plans

What other things could you and your families do to increase your cash flow monthly? Once our emergency fund is established, and once we have begun investing for the future, we can use these extra funds to begin a rapid debt-relief system. Paying your debt off once and for all will always be the best system.

Getting to G.O.O.D.

These are ways to pay yourself or shift funds from one pocket to another.

- Get a second job
- Pay off debt with an equity loan
- Sell stuff
- Do an interest rate swap
- Lower your tax refund by adding exemptions
- Seek professional financial and tax help
- Get rid of high-interest debt first
- Borrow from your 401(k)
- Limit your 401(k) investments to the matching amount
- Consider home refinance as a tax deduction
- Consider a Reverse Mortgage; talk with a licensed, reputable mortgage specialist
- Declare war on debt; it is your enemy
- Make more money. Yes! Find a way to make more money!

Getting to G.O.O.D.

In my experience, some financial problems can only be managed by an increase in income. There is a level where management is the right thing, and there is also a level where your personal earnings are what make the difference.

While adding degrees, and MBA status can help us in the long term, what might you do in the short term (1-3 years) that might radically change your financial future? There are lots of ways to legitimately earn extra money. Here are just a few ideas that might inspire you to "Learn To Earn". First, here is the absolute truth:

> **YOU CANNOT SOLVE A PROBLEM WITH THE SAME KIND OF THINKING THAT CREATED IT**

Consider these ways to add income:

1. Sell things on Craigslist. Seriously. I have met numerous people who have added $200 per month or more just by going to garage sales and reselling neat items on Craigslist or ebay. Buy low and sell high. It is the American way! It requires little start up capital and you could be well on your way by next Saturday!

2. Drive for Uber or Lyft. Drivers report making excellent part time income in this environment and you most likely already own the tools to add extra income: A Smart Phone and a working automobile!

3. Check the list in our childrens job section and realize that ANYONE can do any of these things....it just takes desire and implementation!

4. Consider Network Marketing. Despite many ill-informed opinions, Network Marketing or Multi Level Marketing is real, it is legitimate, and it is here to stay.

Billions of dollars each year are moved through this "Direct Selling" model which has many advantages over traditional business ownership. Generally, the start up fees are very low compared to traditional business or franchising. Often, they are selling well thought out products that benefit people. Here are a few things to consider when contemplating a legitimate network marketing company:

1. Is the product real and is it high quality? Of course, EVERY business should be required to answer this! Ask this of yourself when considering any legit company: WOULD I PERSONALLY BUY THIS PRODUCT FOR MYSELF IF THERE WERE NO COMPENSATION PLAN INCLUDED? If the answer is yes, then you probably are off to a great start!
    If the answer is no, then RUN AWAY!
2. Is it priced fairly? The draw of MLM companies can be that there are few brick and mortar stores, and direct selling in some ways should reduce the consumer cost. So always ask this question: WOULD I BUY THIS PRODUCT AT THIS PRICE IF THERE WERE NO COMPENSATION INVOLVED?
3. Is the company well established and well run? Do I have access to learn about compensation and is there adequate product and sales training?

There are so many fantastic Network Marketing Companies in America and now around the world! MLM is very simply the most direct way to sell products through qualified distributors. It has been spurred on to new heights by tough economic times and a population that strongly desires more time and money freedom.

Winning in this kind of business, like all others, takes persistence, dedication, commitment to education, and a high ethical standard to take care of the client. The long ago worries about the word "Pyramid" are usually unfounded and an unfair representation of something fairly simple.

There are many legitimate companies in Network Marketing, and I am sure there are some unsavory ones as well. That can be true in any industry which is why it takes some research to make sure you are with a reputable outfit. If you are wanting to increase your disposable income at home, get out of debt, or potentially have more free time, the next time someone invites you to take a look, what have you got to lose?

There are a multitude of ways to earn extra money in this country. It may take time and persistence to increase your own cashflow and wealth. Most likely, it will be a process and quite possibly worth it!

Now, Stay Out of Debt!

I realize this is easier said than done. However, look at all the progress you have made in just a few chapters! You no longer overpay your taxes or your phone bill or your insurance premiums. All of these found dollars are now in your budget and should be ample to help you satisfy your monthly requirements. You are truly on your way!

Make a commitment right now to stay out of debt. You and your spouse should make this commitment together. Of course you will want to use credit cards for things like car rental, airline tickets, and some online bill paying. Be cautious in using debt as a way of life, however.

You've just completed the five steps to a solid financial plan. You have discovered the five clues that numerous other wealthy families have used. Implementing these, like most things, is easier said than done. There might be a little pain in giving up old habits.

> **But I assure you the pain of erasing bad habits is substantially less than the pain of living with the results of those same bad habits. There is a cost if you do and a cost if you don't. The cost, if you do change your habits, is voluntary. The cost if you don't change your habits is compulsory.**

Congratulations on completing these five steps. Doing them in order may change your financial life forever! If you have made it this far, I want you to know, sincerely, that the author of this book is very proud of you! Doing crazy things like overpaying your taxes does not make you more patriotic. Living a prudent and thoughtful financial life, however, is one of the most patriotic things you can do. Weak families elect weak leaders. We need strong financial families in this country, and we need them right now. It is your obligation to lift yourself up, dust yourself off, and move forward toward a better life that you alone have designed. Don't cop out and wait for any other human to do this for you. This is on you. Yes, **YOU**!

Remember it is the slight edge that will make all the difference for you. Little things add up to a lot of things. Gaining two extra pounds a year from high school to the age of 50 is a catastrophe.

Ignoring the compound effects of a little bit of money saved over a long period of time, at a reasonable interest rate, is an equal catastrophe. At the end of your economic life, you'll find your tummy to be fat and your wallet to be skinny. To pay your bills, pay for your lifestyle, pay for retirement, and pay for your dreams, you must first have the ability and willingness to _**PAY**_ attention to the little things!

Chapter Eight
Investing in a New Era:

"Pardon Me; Do You Have Any Grey Poupon?"

Rule: ROI Should Stand for Reliability of Income, NOT Return on Investment!

Let's take a trip back in time all the way to 1980

"Pardon me; do you have any Grey Poupon?"

"Who Shot JR?"
- Fans of CBS's *Dallas* television series

"Here's Johnny!"
- Jack Nicholson, in *The Shining*

"No, I am your father" (NOT Luke, I am your father)
- Darth Vader, to a surprised Luke Skywalker

Computer modem invented

Post-It Notes are invented/released

Mount Saint Helens was exploding. The stock market was about to explode in similar fashion. The great questions of the day were, *"Who shot JR,"* and, *"Pardon me do you have any Grey Poupon?"*

The first computer modem was invented. The Post-it note went live. And the beginnings of a new era in investing were upon us.

This was the time when employers were beginning the shift from defined benefit plans (pensions) and the creation of defined contribution plans (IRA, 401(k)). The Dow Jones industrial average was 759 compared to 17,000 as of this writing. A benefits counselor named Ted Banna was deciphering tax code in 1980 and helped create the first 401(k) plan. **Things were about to change in a big way.**

During this time, public access to the stock market was rather limited. Many of the firms that existed were purely for the benefit of the wealthy and didn't have a high service level for the middle class. The fact was not many people had a broker or an advisor during the late 1970s and early 1980s. The creation of the 401(k), the IRA, and the pending accessibility of market instruments through the internet was about to create the perfect wave of market acceptance of individual long-term investing. The current cultural shift was taking place and nobody could stop it.

Fast forward to today in 2015, the majority of working Americans have access to the stock market. Instead of just a handful or a few percent, almost everybody has the availability to buy stocks bonds mutual funds IRAs, Roth IRAs, or can participate in a 401(k) through an employer-sponsored plan at work. The fact is, the market is now available to everybody. On a more interesting note, there are eighty million baby boomers accelerating toward retirement at this exact moment. Nearly 10,000 people a day will be turning sixty-five for the next twenty-two years. What we are witnessing in the stock market, the retirement planning market, and the personal finance world, are the first measurable round of results from the switchover in thinking from company-sponsored plans to individually-funded plans. Round one of the investing wars is over. Take a moment now, look back, and contemplate how well your investment accounts performed.

In this section, we will be introducing three unique viewpoints on investment concepts. We will not be discussing any specific investment, any specific insurance company, or any specific annuity product. Instead, we will look at each of these areas generically that we might leave this chapter with a broad understanding of other alternatives.

How Does It All Work Together?

The money-in-motion flowchart below shows how a typical family might orchestrate their money from the moment they earn it to the moment they invest it. The starting point for the Money-in-Motion Flowchart is money earned (Circle A). This is usually in the form of wages for most people. These dollars usually flow into your checkbook, which is indicated by the arrow to the right.

Circle B is an allocation for actual cash whether you keep it at home, in your wallet or purse, or in a coffee can, buried in the backyard. It is important to have immediately-available cash at all times. The amount can vary, of course, but you will find yourself in situations where your Visa card is no good and you simply need a stack of money to remedy the situation.

Circle C is the reserve account we talk about or your emergency fund. We also call this a "float account." For example, let's assume that you are most comfortable keeping $10,000 in your float account. You have also decided that should this account go below $7,000, you would make certain allocations and changes in order to fill it back up to the original $10,000.

> **This is your financial thermostat.**

Once you earn some money, put some money in your checkbook, stash a little cash, and create a float account, this is the perfect time to accelerate your investment contributions. The four circles below your reserve account represent varying types of investments that you might choose to hold your long-term investments.

Money-In-Motion Flowchart

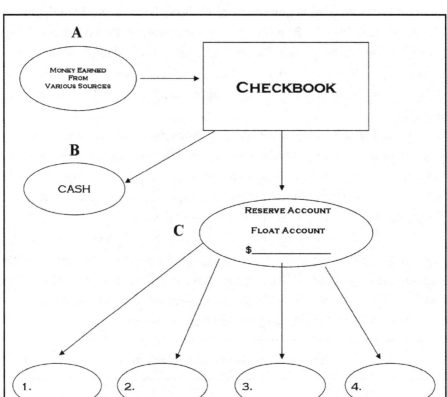

Basic rules of investing

1. Purpose: The dollars that you are investing are for the long-term. There should be little or no consideration of using these resources anytime during the next five years. According to the **Money-in-Motion Flowchart,** you should have ample cash reserves early in the process. Your investment dollars are not for emergencies; these dollars are not to buy a house with; these are long-term dollars

2. We are aware of and are comfortable with the risk of each investment.

We have a keen understanding of the potential downside, we understand the fees, costs, and limitations of the program, and we understand the potential upside limits as well

3. If our financial situation or condition should change significantly, we would make the appropriate changes to our program

4. After my basic long-term investment program is established, I will continue to work toward becoming *bad-debt* free

5. You have a basic understanding of how each of your investments will be taxed during the accumulation time or during the income phase

Three Keys to Your Economic Engine: A Biased Opinion

Before we spend much time discussing alternative investment types, let me be clear and upfront with you: I am biased. So is every other author, advisor, and financial planner. My bias is based on the fact that I love my clients and these three decades of experience need to serve for something positive. Hence, my bias. I want to win for my clients, and that is the epicenter for the bias contained herein.

When many people discuss bias I think they confuse the word with influenced. We are all biased toward things that we prefer. And usually we prefer things that have demonstrated a high level of efficiency and proficiency. However, I am not influenced by any product or company, nor am I influenced by any opportunity to rightfully earn compensation other than in a method that is beneficial for all parties involved.

With that, let's discuss some investment and savings ideas that I believe work very well for most people. There are thousands of mutual funds, stocks, and bonds out there. It is a daunting task to discern which ones are right for you. Which philosophy do you believe in? Buy low, sell high? Buy and hold? Buy high, sell low? Play the lottery?

Chapter Nine
Have Your People Talk to My People:
Actively Managed Accounts

Also called: *actually* managed accounts

Rule: watch over your money or have an expert do it for you

Actively managed accounts. These may go by other names such as privately-managed accounts, but the purpose is the same for either: to be in the right risk category based on my own personal tolerance and to participate in rising markets to some degree while minimizing falling markets.

In general, actively-managed accounts have a *primary* money manager who makes the daily decisions as to where the money is invested at any given time. It can be all stocks, all bonds, the combination of stocks and bonds, certain commodities, baseball cards, ETF's, cash equivalents, or other individual equity positions. These choices are left to a money manager who also has the ability to be *all in* the market or *all out* of the market. Being careful goes both ways.

This strategy is more of a disciplined strategy. Its purpose is to:

- Be an emotionless and mathematical driven process
- Attempt to avoid major market downturns
- Move to cash and/or lower risk investments during market declines
- Since greater capital might be available because it was pulled out of the market during a downturn, there might be opportunities to reinvest during advancing markets

Avoiding market downturns is just the start of an effective risk-management system. Not every actively managed account will yield a profit. Make sure you have adequately assessed your risk tolerance before investing money. Any account in the stock market can lose money including principal.

While active money managers have existed for a long time, they have generally served only the wealthy. In fact, I have seen many examples out in the market where the larger managers and brokerage houses publicly stated that they were only looking for clients with $1 million or more.

I say, "To each his own!" But, really, who is out there offering actively-managed accounts for investors with less than $1 million? In today's market, more and more investment advisors are opting to help clients with investments of varying sizes.

How is this different than most mutual funds? Mutual funds have experienced great popularity since the early '80s and the onset of the 401(k) and the IRA. But who tells you when to get in and when to get out of certain mutual funds? Generally, mutual funds operate and are sold by prospectus. Inside the prospectus you will usually find a statement of purpose for the particular fund you're looking at. This statement of objective will tell you whether or not the fund manager intends to remain invested at all times regardless of the prevailing market conditions. As we have seen in recent years, often, the fund manager must remain invested in the market to some degree *even if the market is headed south.*

Actively-managed accounts do not have the same requirement to adhere to the prospectus. In recent falling markets it was very difficult to explain to clients why the fund manager didn't bail out of certain stock positions and essentially were required by law to remain locked into a falling market. Actively-managed accounts work very differently. The money manager has the right to get in the market and also has the right subsequently to get out of the market based on the prevailing economic conditions.

From a set up and transparency standpoint, I believe these types of accounts are the easiest to establish and understand. Your account is opened by selecting a basic brokerage account with any of the major custodians. (Charles Schwab, Fidelity, Folio Institutional and Ameritrade are all fine examples of custodians). The third-party money manager makes trades within your own account and the entirety of the account ***never leaves your possession***! The money manager has no right to withdraw your funds for any reason other than to collect a pre-arranged and documented management fee.

Simple!

Money University speaks conceptually about actively- managed accounts. Our purpose in this class is not to recommend any particular investment or firm, but to educate you on the concept of actively-managed money versus going online and buying a mutual fund or stock that you hold for ten years. Before you make any type of investment, you should clearly understand the risks fees and objectives of the proposed program. Every investment program that deals with stocks, bonds, funds, and ETF's can lose money. It is important to understand each of these elements prior to making any investment.

Many of the active money managers today operate in a well-articulated team environment where there is oversight on a continual basis. An overlapping team concept might be the right strategy for you in the coming years. Having a full-time team of investment managers allows me to concentrate on the important things in my business, which are my client relationships, family relationships, my health, and the occasional round of golf!

Chapter Ten
Fixed-Indexed Annuities:
Why Coke Hates Pepsi, McDonald's Hates Burger King, and Your Broker Hates Fixed-Index Annuities

Rule: don't lose money in the market during retirement

Fixed-index annuity products . . . just the mention of the word *annuity* in many circles will usually give pause for a frantic internet search looking for, "what's wrong with annuities?" Depending on whom you ask, an annuity is either the spawn of the devil or it is the greatest thing since the iPad. How can there be so many differing opinions on what is ultimately a very simple concept?

I can't speak to the sales literature of every annuity type available in the United States. There are many types of annuities and not all of them are necessarily good, and none of them are necessarily bad. They are just financial products like anything else. Each company that sells annuity products has gone through rigorous financial testing within their appropriate states. Each agent that represents annuity products has gone through vigorous licensing and training requirements, and as evidenced in recent years, the sales of fixed indexed annuities is growing by billions of dollars each year. There must be something to them. Right?

It has been said that when you are a hammer, everything looks like a nail. Depending on whom you ask, the fixed-indexed annuity might be a cure for your investment woes, gray hair, toenail fungus, and bad breath. If you flip your TV on in search for the same answers, you might also hear an opinion that the same annuities **cause** gray hair, toenail fungus, and bad breath. To both sides I would like to offer my extreme version of financial advice:

nanny nanny pooh-pooh to you

If annuities are so great why doesn't everybody own one? And if annuities are so terrible why haven't the state regulators shut them down? The answer is really simple: *financial turf wars*. The insurance industry and the securities industry do not always see eye to eye. They are sometimes like the mongoose and the cobra.

To me, that is a good thing, because it keeps the competition honest. From my perspective, once you understand what a product is and what a product *isn't*, you can make an informed choice based on your own needs.

Or let's try another approach. Given that these products are licensed in every state and given that there are thousands of agents who represent them, let's take a look at how they actually work and make a decision based on the facts as they relate to our own personal situation. Here are the basics of fixed-index annuities.

Generally, fixed-indexed annuity accounts are issued by insurance companies. Each of these insurance companies operates within approved states and in accordance with each state's laws. Individual states have certain financial and regulatory requirements and programs to evaluate the solvency of each company.

Fixed-indexed annuities usually grow relative to the upside of an index such as the S&P 500 Index. Normally, their downside risk is 0% gain during a given twelve-month period. For many risk-adverse retirees, this is the single biggest buying point:

> **With an index annuity you will never lose a dime of principal to the market! Depending on the performance of the underlying index, you may also make a reasonable rate of return.**

Remember the three phases of investing?

- **Accumulation**. This is the time, usually during your working years when you're contributing money to the market on a regular basis; a little bit of risk is okay during this time
- **Income**. This is the period of time often called retirement. During the income phase, the significant loss of principal could be devastating to your long-term plan; in my opinion, index annuities might be suited best to this period as they are absent of any risk from the stock market
- **Distribution**. This is the period of time when you send money to your beneficiaries or estate. Non-IRA money that is owned in your annuity account may pass to your heirs and beneficiaries without the hassle of probate. It's one of the unique features of all annuities, life insurance policies, and certain retirement accounts. If it is your intention to leave money to your beneficiaries privately, without the public inquisition of probate, an annuity may very well be a great option for you

Interest Ratcheting. Once interest is earned in a fixed-indexed annuity, it is credited to your account, usually on an annual basis. Once this interest is earned and credited to your account, it also becomes immune to a downturn in the stock market. I call this the ratcheting effect. Here's an example that will explain it for you:

You have $100,000 in your IRA account and you choose to place it in an annuity. Perhaps during the first year this account earns 4%. On the anniversary date, $4,000 will be credited to your $100,000, so at the end of twelve months, you now have $104,000. That $104,000 becomes the high-water mark for your account and will be the **minimum** account balance moving forward. Starting in your next accumulation year, you begin with $104,000 and it will never be lower than that! Of course, if you make cash withdrawals or have any fees associated with your account, it would reduce accordingly.

Income and/or death benefit riders. Certain annuity products allow the addition, for a fee, of a plan rider that guarantees a specific amount of available lifetime income or a specific death-benefit guarantee for your beneficiaries. Let's take a look at a quick example of how one of these income riders might work:

You purchase a fixed-income annuity with $100,000 at the age of sixty. By the age of seventy, assuming you achieved a 4.5% annual rate of return, your account would have approximately $155,000 in the cash-value column. You might be able to take this as a lump sum of cash if you chose to, but the income rider may also make a provision for you to take a guaranteed annual income from this amount that would last the entirety of your life. For example, let's assume that there was a 5% for life income rider that you executed at the age of seventy based on your $155,000. You could turn on the income and receive a guaranteed lifetime income payment of $7,750 per year or $645 per month, guaranteed for life, regardless of how long you live. Some of these riders also offer joint income protection that covers you **and** your spouse.

Once again, we do not offer specific annuities at **Money University** but we do offer a general and broad explanation of how they might work in your situation. Before purchasing any investment or insurance product, annuity or savings plan, please review your situation with a licensed professional and make a decision based on your own personal desire and situation.

Let's take a look at many of the common points of contention from the "mainstream financial industry." To be fair, each of these points **is** valid. You must compare these points with the upside potential and decide whether or not this type of investing is right for you as you move toward retirement.

Fixed-indexed annuities do not gain 100% of the market. Very true. Once again, I refer you to the three phases of investing. During the income phase, you are usually trying to max out the market. You're no longer focusing on ROI, **_return on investment_** but the new ROI **_reliability of income._** A single major downturn in the stock market could wreck your financial plan. There **are** limits to your rate of return with a Fixed-Indexed Annuity. Given that they protect all of the downside, might it be worth giving up some of the upside to protect yourself? All you need to know is, "Will this potential rate of return meet my goals?" If the possible rate of return will not match up with your goals, then this product may not be the best fit for you.

As you make these decisions, keep in mind that your fixed-index annuity will not experience ANY of the downside of the market either!

There are surrender charges. Yup. Once again, this is true. During the first several years, there is a redemption charge if you fully cancel your contract OR you make a withdrawal of greater than 10% in any one-policy contract year. Many of the modern fixed-index annuities seem to have surrender charges in the 9% range during the first nine or ten years. (Be sure to check the annuity contract for the exact details. These charges could be more or less). Usually, the surrender charges decrease each year you own the contract down to 0% at some point. Remember, these are *"MAYBE FEES."* They don't <u>actually</u> occur at all unless you cancel your entire program or exceed the annual withdrawal allowance.

Given that there is no upfront commission charged when purchasing a fixed-indexed annuity, these *"maybe fees"* may not be as relevant as the naysayers claim. Many annuity contracts allow you to take out 10% of the principal balance each year without any kind of fee. This ought to meet the liquidity requirements for the average annuity purchaser.

When comparing these *"maybe fees"* to your current program, it might be fair to add in all of the *"for sure fees"* that you pay for other types of programs. If you have $100,000 invested where you pay a 1% fee, over the next ten years, you would pay a *"for sure fee"* totaling $10,000. Those are <u>real dollars not "maybe" dollars</u>. The great thing about America is you get to choose.

> **Important: if you do not have adequate cash reserves such as those mentioned in the Flow of Money chart in a previous chapter, you should consider funding that account prior to purchasing <u>any kind of annuity</u>.**

The universal question to be answered whether or not to consider a fixed-indexed annuity is this:

> **Would you be willing to give up <u>some</u> of the market upside to prevent <u>all</u> of the market downside?**

Once you realize you are no longer in the accumulation phase and are now entering the income phase, these questions become easier to answer and the opinion of the mainstream financial sales industry becomes easier to ignore!

Important Disclaimer: when purchasing a fixed-indexed annuity from your advisor, take your time. **Never** purchase a major financial instrument on the first visit with **any** broker, EVER. Nobody wants to be pushed into buying anything, especially when it comes to our life savings!

Chapter Eleven
(Not the kind of Chapter Eleven where we go bankrupt, the kind of Chapter Eleven where we learn something really cool):

Life Insurance: Secrets of the System Revealed!

Rule: Death and taxes are certain. How to prepare for life's worst moment, and also prepare for death (Man, I hope that was funny!)

Play along:
... *Like a good neighbor_____.*
... *You're in good hands with_____.*
... *We Are _____.*
dum dee duh duh duh duh duh!
Now that's Progressive…………..
15 minutes can save you 15% on your car insurance.

Think of all the advertising you have endured during your attempts to watch high-quality television programming. It's everywhere: Flo from Progressive. State Farm. The AFLAC duck quacking in your television set. The Piece of the Rock Prudential Half-Time Scoreboard. *It is everywhere*. The life insurance industry in the United States is one of the largest industries on the planet. In almost every major city on top of every major high-rise building, just look at the sign on top and usually it belongs to either an insurance company or law firm!

In this chapter, we will discuss some alternative uses to life insurance as well as some of the basic uses of life insurance. Regardless of what you think about life insurance, this chapter could be very important to you.

Some Basic Life Insurance Factoids

- Life insurance proceeds, when paid to a beneficiary, are usually income tax-free
- Loans and policy withdrawals taken from a cash value accumulating life insurance policy do not usually incur an income tax
- Term insurance is usually the cheapest form of insurance. However, it expires sooner where certain types of permanent insurance, while more expensive initially, generally lasts much longer through life
- When purchasing certain cash value or permanent type of life-insurance programs, a portion of your premium pays for the raw cost of insurance and policy fees and expenses; the remainder of your premium goes toward the cash value accumulation fund; this account is governed by the contract of your policy and the rules of the underlying insurance company; your rate of return on these accounts may vary
- For this conversation, we will focus on two separate types of insurance: 1: *term insurance* as risk protection and 2: *equity indexed universal life insurance* as a tax advantaged and risk-free alternative to the traditional markets

Why We Need Life Insurance

Dating way back to the 1700s, the earliest uses of life insurance were to compensate families of sailors who died in military exercises. Today, there is an equally practical use for life insurance that most responsible parental units and most responsible married people acknowledge: *in the event of premature death, is there a vehicle that I can purchase that might compensate my family, my creditors, or my business interests as though I am still here?*

In a previous chapter, we learned of the concept of *drawdown*. Drawdown is the amount of money that we can take ***from*** some type of savings or investment account and create annual income.

For example, using a 5% drawdown or withdrawal rate, assuming we had $1 million available, we could draw those million dollars down at a rate of 5% a year. Here is what that means:

$1,000,000 at 5% Withdrawal = $50,000 per year Income

So the concept of "How much life insurance should we buy?" is really very simple. There are just a few questions to be answered prior to buying the right amount of life insurance. Let's use a basic sample here to estimate the appropriate amount of insurance for an average family in today's economy.

Goal:

- Replace annual income of $60,000 per year assuming 5% withdrawal rate (Drawdown rate of 5%)
- Pay funeral expenses of $15,000
- Payoff miscellaneous debts of $10,000
- Completely fund children's education $60,000
- Fund the grieving period for my spouse for one year $60,000

Using drawdown on the $60,000 per year income and a 5% withdrawal rate looks like this: $60,000 \div .05 = $1,200,000

Income Replacement	=	$1,200,000
Funeral Expenses	=	$15,000
Misc. Debts	=	$10,000
Education Funds	=	$60,000
Grieving Period	=	$60,000
My Total Life Insurance Need:		$1,345,000

So, in the event of your premature death, a check would be delivered to your family, completely free of any income taxes, in the amount of $1,345,000. This means that your family could carry on as though you are still there earning an income. **Life insurance steps in if you step out.**

From an expense standpoint, this is a pretty simple concept. Generally, term insurance will take care of the mentioned risks. Term insurance policies can run in five, ten, fifteen, twenty, or thirty-year increments. Every policy is different; so make sure that you check the covenants in the contract to determine what your rights are at the end of the policy term. Usually, the longer the term, the more expensive the premium will be.

Ideally, you get serious about saving money somewhere along the line early in life, and by the time you reach sixty-five or seventy, your financial obligations are met primarily by your savings or retirement plan. Later in life, these responsibilities are met by the economic engine we call retirement and Social Security. Earlier in life, your economic engine is your job. Life insurance is your airbag, should your economic engine immediately cease to run. Done correctly, you'll have plenty of cash later in life so that the loss of your income would be a planned event rather than an unplanned event. All of that makes sense in a perfect world, right?

But this world is not perfect, and we need to have some provision in case we haven't saved the right amount of money by retirement. In that case, we might desire to carry our insurance on much later in life. That is where permanent insurance comes into play. With that, I want to introduce the concept that I created, and believe in, called:

"PERMA TERM"

First, I have always wanted to invent a word. *"Perma Term"* is my word! It isn't a real insurance policy-(yet). It doesn't have a contract. You can't call an insurance company up and buy a *Perma Term* policy, in fact. *Perma Term* is a planning concept where we combine the less-expensive nature of term insurance and the longer-term nature of permanent insurance; in this case, equity indexed universal life. *Perma Term* is a strategy and a decision that you and your financial advisor or insurance agent should make together. In the early years, when you earn less money and have more responsibility, you buy the correct amount of insurance, usually term insurance to cover the majority of your risk.

But with a long-term view in mind, it might be prudent to convert a portion of your term insurance program into permanent life insurance. Now there are many insurance agents who are already doing this concept, and I must say if your insurance agent is doing this, I wholeheartedly applaud them. There are lots of great agents out there and a lot of great companies. Most of the people I have met in the industry during my lifetime are really pretty good people.

How Permanent Life Insurance Works

As mentioned above we make premium payments into our equity-indexed universal life policy. A portion of those premiums goes to pay the face amount or raw insurance premium and policy expenses. The remainder goes toward an accumulation fund referred to as the cash value. The insurance company has a provision called minimum premium that is designed to keep the insurance policy alive based on a minimum contribution from the client. There is also another possible premium called the guideline level premium. This premium is based on face amount and age and can be substantially higher than the minimum premium. The resulting impact of a higher premium is a greater cash value accumulation, meaning more money goes into cash value and a fixed amount goes into the insurance part. These funds can be used during the policy owner lifetime and can be accessed through policy withdrawals and policy loans.

While many of you at this point are throwing up again, that is most likely because of your emphasis on the benefits provided by most life insurance companies. These benefits normally occur only at death. All of your focus has been on the benefits that you might receive upon the unexpected death of a loved one. However, one thing to consider is the living benefits of a life insurance policy.

Let's say that you look at a policy whose minimum monthly premium was $200 a month for a $250,000 face amount. What if I told you that the actual premium was actually $1,000 a month? You might freak out a little bit because the premium is five times originally what we quoted. Is the insurance worth $1,000 a month? Not the insurance portion, no. The "expense" is not an expense in the traditional sense. That extra money is headed toward the cash value component of the policy. We call that *"overfunded permanent insurance."*

One of the neat components of equity-indexed universal life insurance is how the money might grow inside the policy. Without showing you a thirty-six-page report, I can't accurately portray how these programs work inside of one short book. But I can give you some general guidelines on how they might benefit you in the future.

The component of the life insurance policy that adds interest to your cash value account is usually tied to an index similar to the S&P 500. That index has a maximum cap to its earnings on it, but it also has a minimum floor to its minimum earnings. Similar to the fixed-indexed annuity, a great question prevails:

> **Would you be willing to give up some of the upside to prevent all of the downside?**

And what if the worst downside potential was positive 1% or 2%? Many of the caps on these programs hover between 10 and 13%. How would you feel if you knew your life insurance savings account was performing between 2% and 10% a year, no matter what was going on outside the market? From where I sit, and after the epic pullbacks of the markets in 2000, 2001, 2002, in 2008, I bet many of you would feel just great!

Overfunded permanent life insurance programs are not for everybody. When you look into one of these type programs make sure you do it with an advisor or agent who is competent and fluent in this area. I don't recommend that you buy something like this over an 800 number or through the internet. You need on-site competent guidance to make sure you're making the right choices.

So let me give you a quick summary here:

- The portion of your premium that goes into cash value is your money to use as a living benefit while you're still <u>alive</u>
- These dollars will grow in accordance with the market or a market index (usually the S&P) and will never lose a single penny because of a potential market downturn
- Often, they will have a floor (minimum rate of return) of 1% and a ceiling of 10 to 12%. So when the market goes up, you go up, but not all the way. And when the market goes down, you still go up, usually around 1%.

There's one final thing to consider when saving resources inside of equity-indexed universal life policy. When you go to withdraw your money or take a policy loan, the revenue you receive is ultimately **<u>free from the federal income tax</u>**. That is a **<u>REALLY BIG DEAL!</u>** How might avoiding income taxes affect your long-term plan? No market loss. Done correctly, no taxation. It is a great thing in America that loans are NOT taxable. When you buy a new Honda Accord and get a loan to do so, that loan for the car is not part of your income tax. Nor is a policy loan from a life insurance policy. There are many considerations when reviewing this type of program, but for some, it absolutely makes sense to investigate using the strength of the insurance industry to help find steady returns and tax-advantaged savings!

Here are some other options that you have with permanent life insurance:

1. Make tax-free withdrawals from your account in the future

2. Make tax-free policy loans from your account in the future (Mentioned twice on purpose)

3. Cancel the policy and take the entire cash value (may have tax consequences—ask your CPA)

4. Many Universal Life Policies have chronic-care riders that allow you to access the death benefit while living in the event of a chronic-care situation of the policyholder. Check your policy contract for more details, or ask a qualified licensed agent

5. Your cash value will never lose a dime to the marketplace

Your cash value will never lose a dime to the marketplace. Ponder this as you consider your options.

This is not your grandfather's type of life insurance. And it may very well suit you as you seek to provide for your family, protect yourself from the market, and protect you and your family from income taxes!

Remember the majority of your death-benefit insurance is coming from lower-cost term. The permanent portion is an allocation where you overfund the monthly premium and seek minimal protection and maximum cash accumulation!

Perma Term is now copyright protected, and is a wonderful idea! Hey Aunt Dorothy, how about that? I created my own word!

Chapter Twelve
How to Raise Financially-Successful Children

Is school preparing your child for the world they face after graduation?

As a parent, have you ever asked yourself:

1. Am I teaching my children the right things about money?
2. Is there anything I can do right now that might benefit them later?
3. Is their school teaching my children how to survive financially, and to thrive in today's AND tomorrow's economic environment?

What do most parents really want for their children? Many will say, *"I just want them to be happy."* Baloney! Most parents really want their children to have a life that is better than theirs is right now.

You would hate finding them working at a job they dislike like in order to pay the bills. You want your children to have enough cash and financial savvy to be "happy." More importantly, I want my children to be independent financially. This takes a certain type of education around money, finances, entrepreneurship, and other related areas.

There are many types of education we receive in the current educational system:

- *Scholastic Education:* (Schools) this is the ability to read, write, do arithmetic, eat paste (K-1 only), take recess, and perform well on academic achievement tests
- *Professional Education:* (Colleges and Technical Schools). This is when you learn to become a doctor, plumber, lawyer, teacher, or any other bona fide position that you seek after leaving school

- *Financial Education:* (Money University). Learning to survive and thrive financially regardless of where you went to school!

Who is currently providing your children a **Financial Education**? Where does this fit in? Who is teaching our kids about wealth accumulation, taxes, investing, entrepreneurship, and charity?

How do we make sure that our children are not financial failures later in life? Is this the responsibility of the schools? Is this responsibility of the parents?

How Parents See Children and Money:

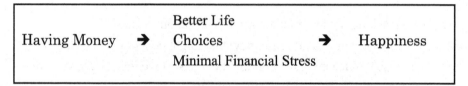

Ironically,

> **Financial success is a key component of how many parents define "happiness" for their children, but few show children how to attain it!**

This chapter may cause you the most pain <u>and</u> the greatest growth. If you have not decided by now to achieve financial success for yourself, perhaps you will do it for your children. Teaching your children may require fixing yourself. Ouch!

Would you like to give your children a great, financial head start? Here are four actions you can take **<u>today</u>** to teach children to be good with money:

1. Start right NOW

2. Put those kids to work!

3. Be encouraging

4. Create Tyke Tycoons

Start Right, Now!

Start teaching children about money at the same age that you teach them to say *please and thank you*, and how to brush their teeth.

Brushing your teeth is a good habit. By repetition, then habit, most of us brush our teeth daily without even thinking about it. Good habits spawn great results. The same is true in teaching your children about money.

It won't be easy, but when was good parenting ever easy?

Establish Positive Financial Attitudes: Money is not "bad," and having money is not "bad" either. Money is merely a tool. Help them believe that anyone can be wealthy. Financial freedom comes from developing the right habits, not from a degree or pedigree.

Your children will develop attitudes and perceptions around money. Make sure they are the right ones. Their mindset is usually formed by you. Be cautious in how you portray money in your own family.

Communicate: Talk to your children about money, or someone else will be the first one to do so. You might not like their advice. Money is a topic that your children will listen to you about.

Don't be afraid. Parents are often afraid to talk to their children about money because they aren't confident in their own financial skills. It is okay that you are not an expert. It is okay that you have made financial mistakes. Don't dwell on your mistakes! Use your experiences as examples for how to fix mistakes and to learn together.

Habits: Stop buying them so much stuff! Say "*no*" to frivolous purchases and "YES!" to opportunity and education! Show your children that they can have luxuries once they can earn them. How will they get money for nicer things? Well, let's look at point two:

Put Those Kids to Work!

Children of all ages can get what they want and need by earning money. As Pink Floyd once said, *"How can you have any pudding if you don't eat your meat?"* Why should children have luxuries if they haven't earned them? When kids earn their own money, they look at cash through new eyes. Jobs create opportunities for children to learn so many new skills, such as interacting with others, marketing, and finance. They gain self-confidence.

Create earnings goals. *"I will make $200.00 this holiday season."* *"I will earn $1,000 to spend on my favorite overnight summer camp."*

Here Are Thirty Opportunities for Children from Ages Four to Eighteen to Earn Money:

1. Babysitter
2. Vending machine owner
3. Pet sitter
4. Do chores for neighbors
5. Lawn mower
6. Camp / Event counselor
7. Weed / yard work
8. Recycle scrap metal
9. Dog walker
10. Gift Wrapper
11. Retail
12. Lifeguard
13. Pet Cage / Tank Cleaner
14. Family business participant
15. Cook dinner once a week
16. Write a neighborhood news column
17. Book reviewer
18. Make and sell how-to videos
19. Auto cleaner
20. Collect, then sell clothes to consignment shops

21. Bus boy (or girl)
22. Make and sell crafts (hats/scarves, jewelry, candy, gift baskets)
23. Garbage can mover
24. Craigslist/ebay organizer or salesperson
25. House cleaner
26. Author an e-book or blog about your favorite subject
27. Taxi Service for high-schoolers
28. Tutor—school, computer, etc.
29. House Sitter
30. Host events (Pumpkin Carving and Gingerbread House Decorating)

One of my former neighbors hosted a "parents-night out" once a month. For $20 per child, I dropped my children off in our neighborhood and had a well-deserved date night! Our children got to play with their friends in supervised games, eat pizza, and be doted on by teenagers. The two male teenage-boy hosts raked in over $100 (after expenses) each time, and their mother knew exactly where they were those Saturday nights. That took babysitting up a notch.

Here is another great example of allowing children to excel:

A friend's daughter paid for one of her overnight summer camps by selling crocheted gloves. She crocheted a set of gloves with a matching scarf for her mother. A woman approached my friend in a restaurant and asked where she had gotten the lovely scarf. She contracted the eleven-year-old girl to sell a version of the scarf in her shop. Many tweens sell their handcrafted wares at local fairs.

Handmade gifts sell. I know four-year-old boys who are awesome house cleaners. They dust, pick up, and vacuum. Best of all, they are cheap and don't ask for health insurance or other benefits!

Be Encouraging, Failure Isn't Possible at This Stage

The best part of this endeavor is to create a fun atmosphere for a child to participate. Kids don't know much about business, so this is their training ground to form their first thoughts and business ideas. Most children aren't capable of making business decisions, so you will have to pitch in frequently. Don't measure their first endeavors by anything other than fun. Also, involve your children in the day-to-day activities of running your household. This will provide them amazing life skills that schools aren't teaching either.

Start small by having them pay some bills with you. Have your child write the checks or reconcile transactions on the computer. Pick one piece of your bill-paying process and have your child do that. Being involved early will help them establish patterns for later in life. Discuss money frequently with your kids, but in a positive light!

Have them help plan your next vacation or event. Have your kids help pick out the place or review costs. Let them brainstorm ways to create some type of business or chore they can do to earn extra money to help with the vacation! Assign a small part of the vacation budget to them. Let your children be involved! It is vital for kids to know that they can and should be involved with the finances. This builds long-term confidence.

Then, when YOU are finally ready, put your child in charge of a portion of their own finances. Don't be afraid to let them mess up a little bit. They are going to mess up. Let them save up to buy something significant to them. Let them be in business FOR themselves, but not BY themselves.

Temporary failure is an excellent teacher. Successful people rarely repeat big mistakes. Keeping your children involved will create higher levels of awareness and responsibility for your whole family. It will reduce the stress that comes with ambiguity. This approach gives you, as parents, the ability to focus on more substantial issues, as well as the freedom and space for incredible family experiences.

Create Tyke Tycoons

Miriam-Webster says that a tycoon is "a business person of exceptional wealth and power." I could not find one definition that said a tycoon had to be a middle-aged adult! We learned about the high cost of waiting in Chapter One. So far in this chapter, you taught your children how to make money and then how to manage it. The final step is multiplying it. Why make them wait to invest?

If you are old enough to spend money, you are old enough to invest it. Products such as Actively Managed Accounts are available from the day your child is born by setting up a Custodial Account for the benefit of the child. Both of my children have Actively Managed Accounts inside an UGMA, Uniform Gift to Minor Account. We talk about this stuff, even if it goes over their head.

Help your children think of themselves as business tycoons. One of my greatest moments came last summer when my oldest daughter came to me and said, "Dad, I need you to show me how to make $200 next month. I have an event to go to, and I need to make enough money to go." I was so proud. She could have come to me and just asked for the money. I would have said *no*, of course.

Having children understand the role of earning money and profits is a behavior that will yield lifetime benefits! Remember, success only comes BEFORE work in the dictionary! Kids today desperately need to know this fact!

So, Cash, you haven't mentioned the "A" word—allowance. Ah allowance. To give or not to give? You will need to pick an allowance strategy. Your decision should be consistent with the steps above. If you want them to earn money, tie allowance to jobs around the house or for your business. If you want to give your children "job-free" or "chore-free" money, have them pay for some of their own expenses, such as fancy shampoo, celebrity-designed jeans and shoes.

Anything educationally that advances your children both as small business owners or as good stewards of money may be rewarding. We created a class just for kids between the age of eight and fifteen called **VBS...Vacation Business School.** This week-long class involves children in starting and running a business, making a profit, and going through the day-to-day steps of basic entrepreneurship. **(www.vacationbusinessschool.com)**

At the end of the day, the best investment you can make in your children is time. You'll never regret spending more time with your kids.

Planning for My Children's Education

Answer "The Big Question" Before Saving for College

As we mentioned at the start of the chapter, there are three kinds of education you should pursue with your children. The first is ***Scholastic Education*** where we learn the basics of reading, writing, and arithmetic. The second type of education we call ***Professional Education*** such as colleges or trade schools. The third type of education that is missing in most families is **Financial Education** where we learn to create, manage, and acquire wealth.

While most communities provide excellent public school educations, you may also choose to send your child to a private school of your choosing. Private school can cost anywhere from $5,000 per year all the way up to $25,000 per year! If this happens to be your choice, your financial plan must accommodate for these expenses. Often, private school can cost more than college.

And what about college for your child? Should you start some type of college savings program for your child? I could write an entire separate book on this topic given the many variables to consider. And with all the variables that exist in college planning, there are even more variables in how to actually save for college.

The Big Question

There are a multitude of college savings programs. From the education IRA to the 529 plan, parents everywhere concern themselves with providing a secondary education for their children. Please know that I'm a huge advocate for education. It is had an enormous impact on my own life. I absolutely support it. However, paying for education can be a complex question, thus, **"The Big Question."**

> **Do you want to start a *college savings plan* for your child or would you rather just have the money available to pay for college?**

These are two very different things. College savings plans are specific instruments with a specific end use in mind. I am not saying that they are good or bad. But I am a control freak of sorts, being the father of two girls. I just don't feel right leaving those kinds of resources to an eighteen-year-old child as we navigate the choppy waters of education.

For me, it is very simple. I just want to make sure that I have the resources available to pay for my child's college. It isn't necessary that those funds come from a college-specific account. The college or university certainly doesn't care where the check comes from. They just want to make sure that the check clears! My personal choice for my children has been to establish the types of accounts mentioned in Chapter Eleven.

These accounts are easy to start, easy to manage, can't lose any money, are income-tax free, and do not show up on the dreaded FAFSA report! Plus, as their daddy, I retain full ownership as long as I choose to. And if my children choose not to go to college, I can transfer these accounts into their name at some point later in life with no complications.

So, college funds? Not for me. Money set aside for college? Absolutely, it is a priority for me. However, controlling these accounts myself is important also.

What If My Child Wants an MBA?

Currently in the USA there are nearly four million people enrolled in an MBA program. By my own calculations, it could cost nearly $100,000 to get an MBA. I was speaking with one of my clients who is a teacher and her school district is requiring her to get an MBA. Once she gets her required degree, her income will go up a measly $9,600 per year! As a money guy, I simply do not understand the math.

You give up three years of your life and $100,000, all for an extra $800 per month? If that makes sense to you, then by all means, prepare your financial plan to include these extra expenditures. I am not being critical, just mathematical! And that leads us to another big question:

> **What if I have to choose between college for my child and retirement for me?**

Choose retirement for you. By the time your child is college age, you are usually in your forties or fifties and have less time to prepare and plan for your own retirement. The child is eighteen to twenty-two years old and has their entire life in front of them. Remember, time is the most important element to your financial success and that of your children. It comes down to this value judgment: would you rather your child struggle a *little bit* during the four years of college, or would you rather struggle a lot during the forty years of retirement?

Summary:

- Education is good. It will make a difference. Make sure you cover all three types of education, Scholastic, Professional, AND Financial
- Education is expensive. However, if you think education is expensive, you should see the cost of NOT getting an education!
- I believe that the parents should have an MBA (MASSIVE BANK ACCOUNT) prior to the children spending any more of the parent's money
- You are almost complete with the first course at Money University. You are on your way!

Chapter Thirteen
Fiscal Fitness at Every Age

Rule: Decide your path and never look back

Mark Twain once said, "You could learn to like a hot stove if you sit on it for long enough." Unfortunately, for many Americans, the financial game and its lack of perceptible rules are almost more than they can bear. Ultimately, most just sit there and do nothing.

There comes a time in every person's life where the situation requires a big decision from them. Perhaps this is that moment for you! Perhaps this book is nothing more than an obligatory read because you were in my Aunt Dorothy's bridge club in 1969 and she made you *promise* to pray for me and support me. Regardless of how you found this book or why you read it, the best time to fix something that is broken is **right now**.

There will be a multitude of questions that you will ask or have already asked. The purpose of conversation and debate is to come to a final conclusion and put the matter to rest. With that, I want to share the top ten questions that I have received on a regular basis over the past thirty years. I figured they must be relevant, because people keep asking them!

F.A.Q. University
The Top Ten List of Client Questions

1. At what age should I take Social Security? Sixty-two, sixty-six, or seventy?

2. How much should I contribute to my 401(k) plan at work?

3. Should I start college savings plans for my children?

4. I don't have any money or any wealth, should I get a will too?

5. I want to pay my house off early. Is it okay if I just send in $200-a-month extra toward my mortgage?

6. I only have enough money to do one thing. Should I plan for my retirement or set money aside for my children's college?

7. My children are almost teenagers. I have zero dollars saved for their college. What should I do?

8. Should I get out of credit-card debt before I start saving for the future?

9. I have an old 401(k) from a previous employer. How should I handle this?

10. Will there be Social Security for me someday?

These are all excellent questions asked by wonderful people. If you have a financial question, it's important that you get it answered in the right way that satisfies your inner curiosity. I encourage you to seek these answers. Whether you use an accountant, CPA, financial advisor, stockbroker, or insurance agent, make sure you get a credible answer regarding your questions. Below, in the F.A.Q. section, are simple remedies, all based on decades of implementation.

F.A.Q. UNIVERSITY

1. At what age should I take Social Security? Sixty-two, sixty-six, or seventy?
There are many factors in considering what age to take Social Security. If you take it at age sixty-two, there are income-earning limits that might detract from your benefit. If you're still working at age sixty-two and making less than $15,000 a year, perhaps taking Social Security might make sense at that point. Remember, the longer you defer taking Social Security, the higher your monthly payment will be.

Conversely, the longer you defer taking your Social Security payments, the less money you have in the bank at that time. Just consider this: let's say you are asking whether you should take Social Security at age sixty-two or wait until age seventy. Let's assume your age-sixty-two Social Security check would be $1,350 per month, and your projected age-seventy check would be $2,000 per month (fictitious numbers, check your own statement). Of course, the $2,000 per month would be nice. But *what did you give up to attain it*? You gave up eight years of $1,350 per month. That's ninety-six months of $1,350 per month. If you took the early Social Security and stuck that money in a coffee can for the following ninety-six months, how much cash would you have in your coffee can? The answer? **$129,600!**

So here's the question: choose one of the following for your age seventy:

1. $1,350 per month in Social Security revenue and $129,600 in the bank to spend as you please, or to leave to your beneficiaries
2. $2,000 per month that expires when you do

Which one did you choose? Depending on how you choose to use your hard-earned benefits, there are always two possible sides.

2. How much should I contribute to my 401(k) plan at work?

Match the match. If the match is 3%, then contribute 3%. You might consider investing all other dollars outside of your company-sponsored plan. You'll have more flexibility and control and ought to be able to create a plan that benefits you.

3. Should I start college savings plans for my children?

Do you want a college savings plan or money for college? They are two very different things. Your children will have more time to recover from a bad college plan than **you** will have in recovering from a bad retirement plan. Your kids can get government assistance, loans, grants, work programs, or go to school part-time. You can't be retired part-time! I believe your overriding objective should be wealth building, and that money doesn't necessarily need to be segregated for college. For me, I would never let my eighteen-year-old daughter somehow be in control of $100,000 in college funds. I know what I might've done with that money at the age of eighteen! If you start early enough, and plan diligently, proper wealth building will give you an advantage when planning for college.

4. I don't have any money or any wealth, should I get a will too?

Absolutely, right away. Everybody eighteen years of age and older should have a will, medical power of attorney, directive to physicians, and any other legal document that help your family in the event you become incapacitated.

5. *I want to pay my house off early. Is it okay if I just send in $200 a month extra toward my mortgage?*

Usually no. Once you put money into your equity, you can never get it out again unless you sell or refinance the house. Why not use that $200 a month in true wealth building and begin some type of meaningful long-term savings program?

There is no rate of return on equity. Equity is not liquid. You can't even buy a cup of coffee with equity.

6. *I only have enough money to do one thing. Should I plan for my retirement or set money aside for my children's college?*

Planning for retirement is the first essential thing you should do with money. As mentioned above, your children can get loans or make other provisions for college. It's okay to be on government assistance of some sort while you're in college, but it is definitely not okay to be on government assistance while you are retired.

7. *My children are almost teenagers. I have zero dollars saved for their college. What should I do?*

It sounds like you should take a serious look at your financial life. Talk with a trusted advisor, or your pastor, or your CPA, and make a plan to accumulate the right amount of money. It may involve you going back to college **first** and getting a better job. You may have to adjust your lifestyle right now. There is no easy answer for "*How do I pay a big bill with no money?*"

8. *Should I get out of credit-card debt before I start saving for the future?*

No. The high cost of waiting to save is just too high. Use this time to create a new habit that will carry you into the future. If you never get started saving for the future, you will remain unprepared for this path that we are all on. Getting out of debt normally comes as the fifth step of your financial plan.

9. *I have an old 401(k) from a previous employer. How should I handle this?*

First, you may consider rolling your old 401(k) plans into your own personal individual retirement account. It will give you more control, and you might be able to make additional contributions to it sometime in the future. Another consideration would be to evaluate whether or not you should convert your individual retirement account into a Roth IRA retirement account. Roth IRA accounts are not taxable during retirement (Income Phase) and may offer a better prospect for accomplishing your goals in the future.

10. *Will there be Social Security for me someday?*

I sincerely do believe so. I believe the government will make the right kind of arrangements and allocations to protect the Social Security program. It doesn't mean that they're running it perfectly, but I do believe they will make the right choices in the years to come. If you're truly worried about it, get serious about making your own way financially, and make decisions **right now** as though Social Security might not be here. And when you get to age sixty-six and find that the system is still here, wouldn't that be a great blessing?

I truly love answering these questions. Right now, with all the demands of life and economic worry that we have endured, many people are uneasy about the future. But I am an optimist. I'm an optimist because these things are in our control. They are in *your* control. Once you've made up your own mind about how your future must look, things will change for you and do so in rapid fashion.

I believe in the dreamers. I believe in entrepreneurs. The United States is still the greatest nation on the planet, and I believe that our best has yet to come. During the past several years, our country has suffered economic upheaval and has been brought to her knees. But slowly, one person by one person, we are standing up, we are getting stronger, and we will prevail. Your decision to become financially independent is one of great practicality and even greater patriotism. Weak families elect weak leaders. Weak people are preyed upon. Each of us has something inside of us that tells us to stand up and be counted. Reading this book and taking the instruction is one such step. I hope you make this step count.

Why Politics Don't Matter

When was the last time the President or your Congressman sent you a check, paid your bills, or dropped your kids off at school for you? Never? Right! And I suspect that whoever the President is in the future, you don't need to wait around for them to help you directly. I would suggest that an ideal world would be one where neither you nor I really cared who the President was. Because our country is under great stress, it seems like our political leaders are more relevant than they really are, and they are certainly more relevant than they were designed to be!

Let's make ourselves bulletproof. Let's set our families up in such a way that we are mostly immune to the craziness that comes out of Washington D.C.. Our country needs to restore our national sense of pride and that begins with strong families. I am proud of YOU for making it this far. Decide right now that YOU are "The President of Your Own Family" and that YOU will dictate economic policy into your own house! You are powerful and make great decisions. Reading this book is proof of that!

Chapter Fourteen
Putting It All Together; Final Thoughts:
If You're Tired of Starting Over, Stop Quitting

Rule: Carry on my wayward son; don't stop believing

This was one of those moments. All my years of hard work in high school, all my studying, my relentless pursuit of excellence, the great advice from relatives, the encouragement and mentorship from my teachers, and the example set for me by my parents had led me to this one specific moment where it all came together.

There I was, about to take the next big step in life. My 1964 Ford Fairlane was packed and ready for college and I was on my way!

My dad stepped out to give me his last few tidbits of manly advice on the journey in front of me. I know he had been preparing for this moment himself probably since he found out my mom was with child. I couldn't tell if he wanted to hug me or not, but it seemed like quite possibly the inside of his manly exterior was really just another sentimental dad, pushing the baby bird out of the nest. I noticed he had something green and folded in his hand and I could tell he was about to give it to me. I was so excited! My dad shook my hand and gave me the proceeds he had been holding carefully all these years and said the following to me:

"Son, you're not totally worthless. At least you can serve as a bad example. Oh yeah, on your way back from your remedial math class at community college, would you use that five dollars I gave you and stop and get me a barbecue sandwich?"

This is a moment I will always cherish. And to be honest, there is much to be learned here. My parents taught me to be fiercely independent and to rely on nobody else for my success and that I alone would be responsible to make my own way through this world. We were each given a life to make something with. On that day, I learned two very important lessons: 1) if it is to be, it is up to **me**. 2) In 1979, you could buy three barbecue sandwiches for five dollars, and if you played it just right, you could take care of lunch and dinner with careful "planning."

So here we sit at the crossroads of your next major journey. Your financial vehicle and your economic engine are running smoothly, you have a clear destination in mind, the tank is fueled, the insurance is paid in advance, and your map is clearly detailed. I don't believe that God makes any junk. Your life matters. Your finances matter. Your level of comfort and achievement matter, at least to me.

I find that regret comes in many forms. To me, the worst kind of regret is when somebody says, "*I wish I had....*" Very rarely do I hear, "*I'm sorry that I did.*" Take these moments with your spouse or significant other and deal with your finances. Get it right this time. You're truly meant to do great things. But it is up to you, it always has been. You got this. Let's get started.

Definitions

Accumulation phase: the time of your life when you are most actively saving new dollars; usually between the ages of twenty-five and sixty-five.

Income phase: this is the time of your life where you are spending down your retirement and pension programs; no new income is coming in normally during this phase.

Distribution phase: this is when you send your money and assets to the next person in line—usually right before or after death.

Drawdown: a planned percentage amount of withdrawal from an account; if you had $100,000 and used a 4% drawdown, you would take approximately $4,000 per year from your investment.

Retirement rate of return: an objective rate of return that you might shoot for during the retirement years.

ROI (Return on Investment): the amount of money you earned on your investment account.

ROI (Reliability of Income): your ability to take certain retirement assets and turn them into income-producing accounts; these accounts may be held in less-volatile types of accounts to reduce the risk of principal loss.

Gob of Cash: gob of cash.

Qualified plan: certain retirement-type accounts for which taxes have not yet been paid; it is usually taxable with every withdrawal. Examples: IRA, 401(k), etc.

Nonqualified plan: varied taxation; can be taxed annually or on the earnings of capital gains and dividends; has no tax-preferential treatment.

Roth IRA: not tax deductible on the front end; tax FREE on the back end.

Traditional IRA: tax deductible on the front end; fully taxable on the back end.

Baby boomer: you, or your parents—most likely born after WWII through 1964; about 80,000,000 US Citizens are considered baby boomers; 10,000 per day will turn sixty-five for the next twenty-two years.

Annuity: savings contract issued by an insurance company; usually tax deferred if non-qualified; can hold IRA assets also.

Life insurance: risk-management tool as well as savings vehicle; in its most simple form, it pays a check to a named beneficiary in the passing of the policyholder or insured.

Mutual fund: pooled and managed investment, sold by prospectus, with a stated objective; can be qualified or non-qualified, IRA, 401(k).

Stock: ownership of a company.

Bond: a structured loan to a company; corporate debt.

Privately-managed account: actively-managed account; flexible-management style.

Inflation: prices and costs are going up and the impact on your life.

Financial emergency: an emergency that money can fix.

Macho Man: a man who knows it all, ignores danger and death, and is afraid of nothing—resembles Superman, but usually turns out to be Supper Man.

Web Addresses That Can Help You!

www.moneyuniversitythebook.com

www.isavea2z.com
This is a great site that includes up-to-date information on all kinds of good deals for families.

www.vacationbusinessschool.com
Free weeklong summer class for kids eight to fifteen. Has an emphasis on entrepreneurship, and the basics of business. Did I mention that it is a FREE class during the SUMMER?

www.asamanthinketh.com
Written in 1909, this is one of the great, enduring works in the field of personal development.

Social Media:
Facebook.com/moneyuniversitythebook
Twitter.com/moneyubook
Instagram.com/moneyuniversitythebook
Pinterest.com/moneyuniversity
Plus.google.com/moneyuniversitythebook
Youtube.com/channel/moneyuniversity

Bonus Chapter
When Tithing is a tight thing

Perhaps we should have visited this chapter first. The financial concept of giving, also called tithing, has a Biblical basis. Our country has a charitable heart. So many organizations are supported and funded by charitable giving. This giving concept is not just prevalent in the church; universities, not for profit organizations, and other worthwhile endeavors significantly rely on the kindness and cheerful giving of people.

In this section, we will examine some fun and unique ways that you can give. A recent experience at my church caused me to wonder, "What goes on in the mind of a person being asked to give?" This thought occurred to me during the portion of our service we call the offering. God calls us to be cheerful givers. As I looked around the church I realized that there might be several people who genuinely have a heart for giving, but may not have the financial ability to do so. What then?

Is it possible that there might be other ways for you to become a cheerful giver? And whether your ability is high or low when it comes to giving, the following ideas may expand your thinking when it comes to living a charitable life. Given a little bit of insight, you can enjoy a wonderful charitable life, and enjoy helping people and organizations reach their potential.

1. TIME. I have always believed that time is more valuable than money. Whatever the organization, they can always use somebody who's willing to put their hands on a project. Perhaps you could help out in a child care at your church, or by passing out flyers in your neighborhood. One of the simplest things we can do is offer our time to somebody. I believe that one of the greatest things you can do with another human is to simply spend some time with them. There are so many great organizations in this country: meals on wheels, habitat for humanity, Salvation Army, or your local homeless shelter. Any of these organizations would gladly welcome your gift of time.

2. TALENT. Perhaps you could be a speaker for an organization as a fundraiser. Maybe you could help build a new shelf in the kitchen of the local women shelter. Using your talents and abilities is a wonderful way to provide much needed service. What would it be like for you if you donated an hour a week to a worthy cause? I think it would be amazing! In fact this might be better in some instances than just sending a check. Imagine the relationships that could be created and the friends that you might make.

3. SUPPLIES. My family supports a local dog shelter. I love dogs and all animals. They always need extra dog food blankets brushes and leashes. Of course they need money too, but I have never been turned away when showing up with a case of dog food. Ask your local charity how you can help provide them with necessary supplies. I often find these supplies at garage sales and I'm always happy to pick them up cheaply on behalf of my furry friends.

4. CORPORATE MATCHING PROGRAMS. This is one of the best tithing concepts I have seen in a long time. There are many corporations with a heart for giving in this country. You will want to ask your human resources department if such a program exists. In these programs the corporation will match a certain percentage of your own giving effectively doubling your intended gift!

5. PERSONAL FUND RAISERS. There are so many different ways to raise money. We have all pitched in to buy Girl Scout cookies, to buy candy and popcorn from the local school, and to donate our change to the various organizations who need our help. In fact one of the changes you can make in your giving strategies is to take all of that change you have saved and donate that as your gift.

Another way to create personal giving is to do some type of fundraiser where you ask your local community to participate. A bake sale, garage sale, or the donation of an old vehicle all count when it comes to giving. What are some of the great and creative things you could think of that you and your friends could do to support your favorite charity? With YOU, the possibilities are endless.

6. PRO BONO SERVICES. Free gifts of service. Perhaps you work for a corporation that could provide some type of help for a charitable organization. Maybe you know a plumber or electrician who also have a heart for service and would be willing to support your group. It never hurts to ask and you won't know until you do.

7. GIFTING OF LIFE INSURANCE. During their working years life insurance is an essential part of any financial program. What about those times after the kids are grown, the debts are paid, and you may no longer need as much life insurance coverage? Because life insurance is sold for pennies on the dollar, you allocating life insurance proceeds to charity may be a fantastic way to help meet both yours and your charities long-term goals.

Many life insurance policies can be converted into a paid up for life status. Check with your personal insurance agent or financial advisor to understand all of the rules and regulations and state compliance issues with any change like this. How cool would it be to donate a fully paid-up insurance policy to your church?

There are so many ways to give. One thing that really helped me as an adult was when I finally realized how wealthy we all are in this country. There are so many places on this planet that don't have electricity or ice cubes or the internet or televisions. Yet, even in our poorest neighborhoods these things are all prevalent. We have it great here in the USA. God truly did bless the United States of America. And once you realize how wealthy you already are relative to the rest of the world, you can truly count your blessings and begin to focus on other people.

If you are a giver by nature you probably know so many more ways to give than the few mentioned here. I believe we are in a period in our country where simply loving one another would solve so many problems that currently seem insurmountable. God tells us to be cheerful givers! Giving is not an obligation it is a privilege and a great way to say thank you for this blessed life we all live.

Cash Matthews is a licensed financial advisor who lives and works in Austin, Texas. Since the early 80's, he has worked with families on the significant issues we all face in life: Retirement planning, debt management, investing, insurance, income strategy, as well as entrepreneurship and small business development. He also created Money University, The Class, Vacation Business School (VBS) for kids, The Business Owners Network for Entrepreneurship, and is the author of "The Solomon Way", an industry training manual for financial advisors. Outside of his business career, in 2006, he was inducted into the National BMX Hall of Fame, located on the grounds of the United States Olympic Training Facility in Chula Vista, California. He is married with two children, and still loves to ride bikes with his friends!

Whether you want to purchase bulk copies of
Money University
or buy another book for a friend, get it now at:
www.moneyuniversitythebook.com

CPSIA information can be obtained
at www.ICGtesting.com
Printed in the USA
FSOW04n1442240616
21980FS